# With Different Eyes

mke Braselmann

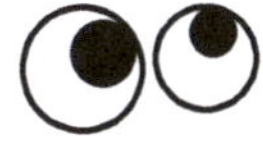

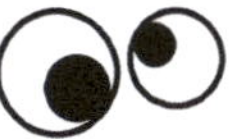

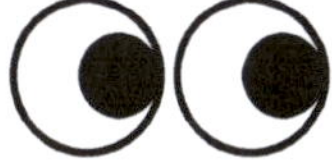

o You See What Eye See? - Volume 1

book with creative pictures that will open your eyes to the little things.

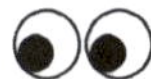

With Different Eyes
Do You See What Eye See? -  Vol.1

© 2016 Imke Braselmann
1. edition


More information and products at:
www.MitAnderenAugen.eu

More books at www.amazon.de

# With Different Eyes

There is so much to see if you just open your eyes and look around.

Everywhere you look, in scuffs and stains, on trees and stones, on the street and in forests, you can find things that look like faces or animals.

This phenomenon is called Pareidolia. Not everyone can see these creatures, but with a pair of googly eyes at the right spot, it's a lot easier.

Try it out and see the world "with different eyes"!

*The next time you go outside,*
*Look for the creatures, 'cause they hide.*

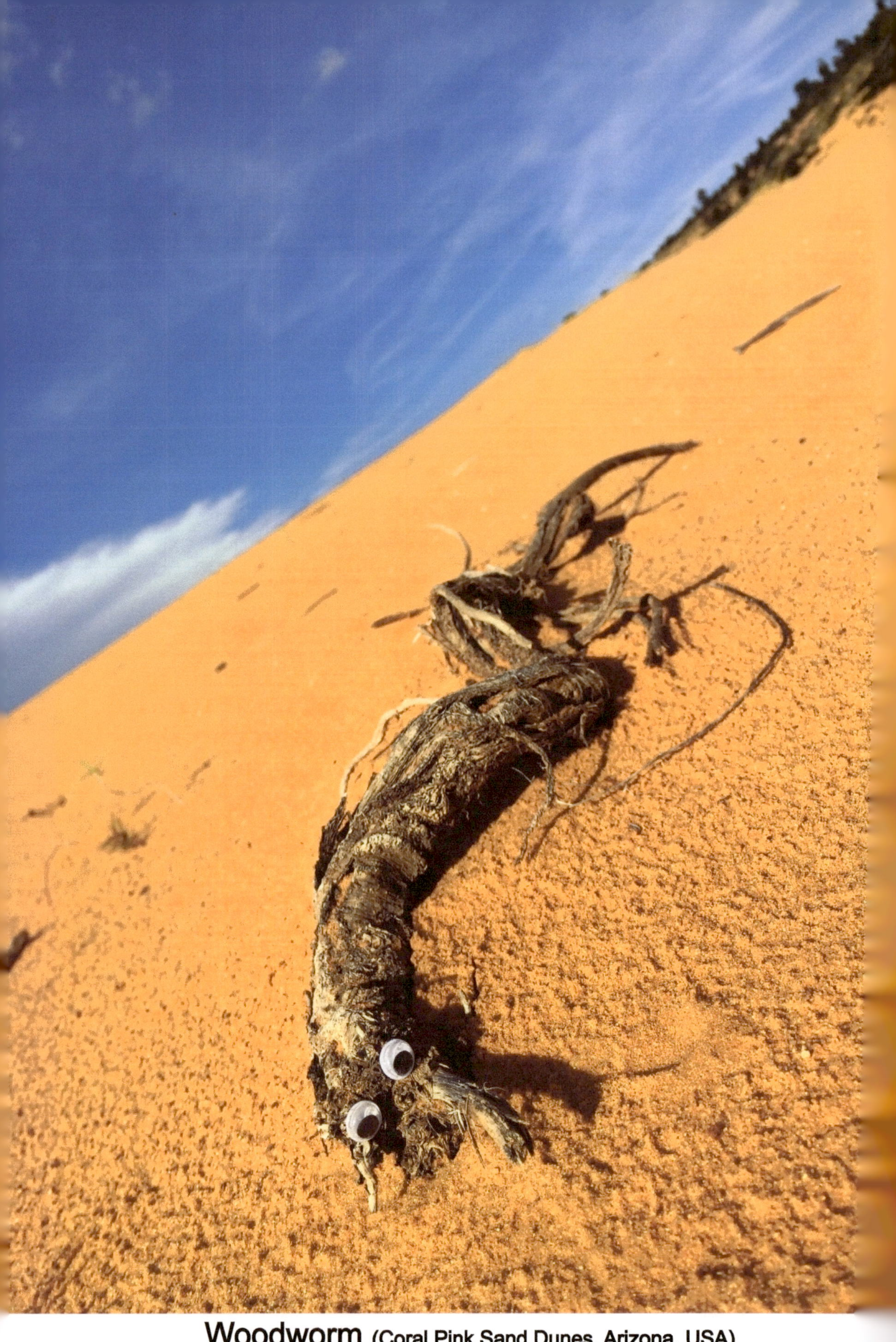

**Woodworm** (Coral Pink Sand Dunes, Arizona, USA)

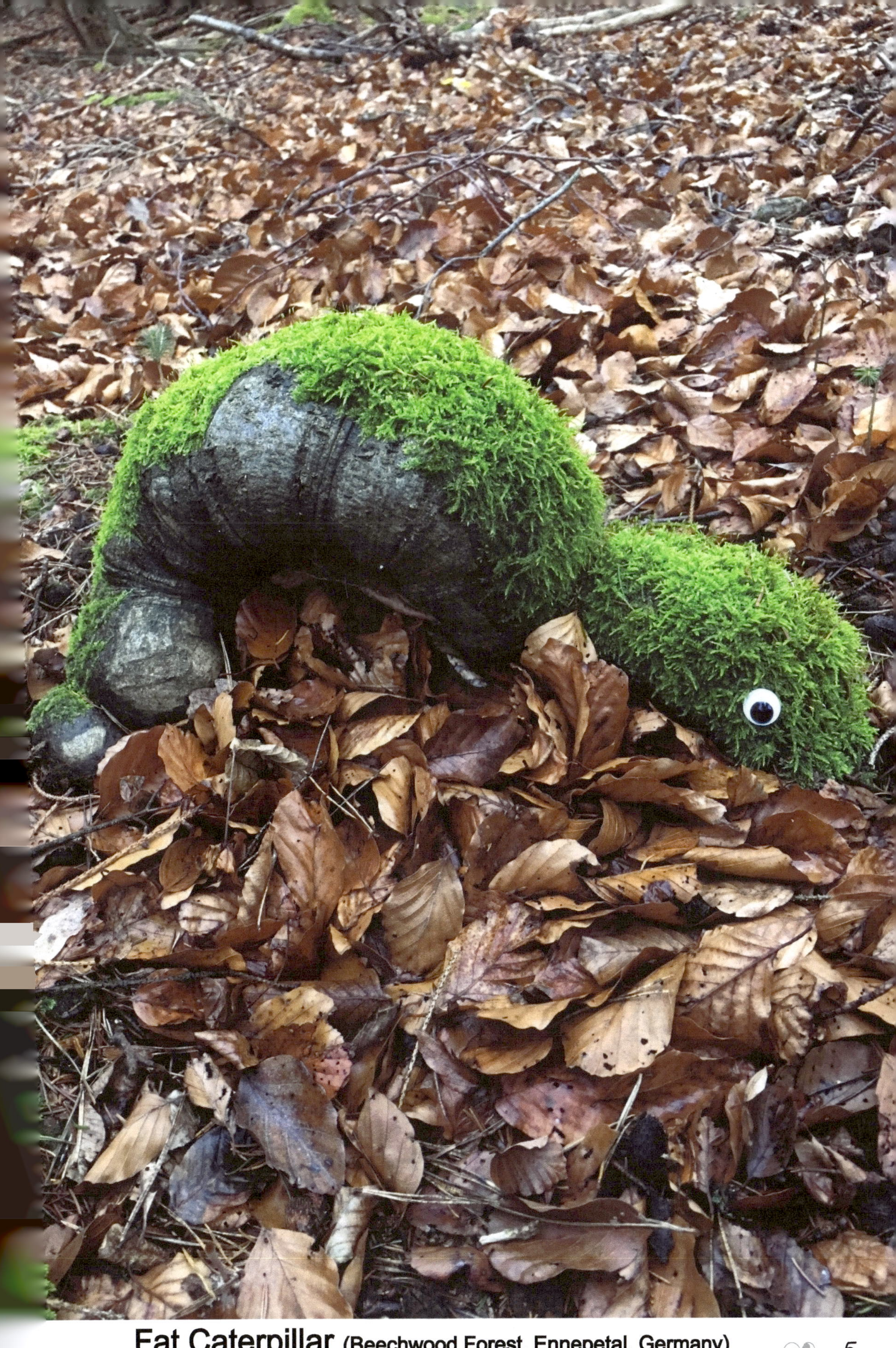

**Fat Caterpillar** (Beechwood Forest, Ennepetal, Germany)          5

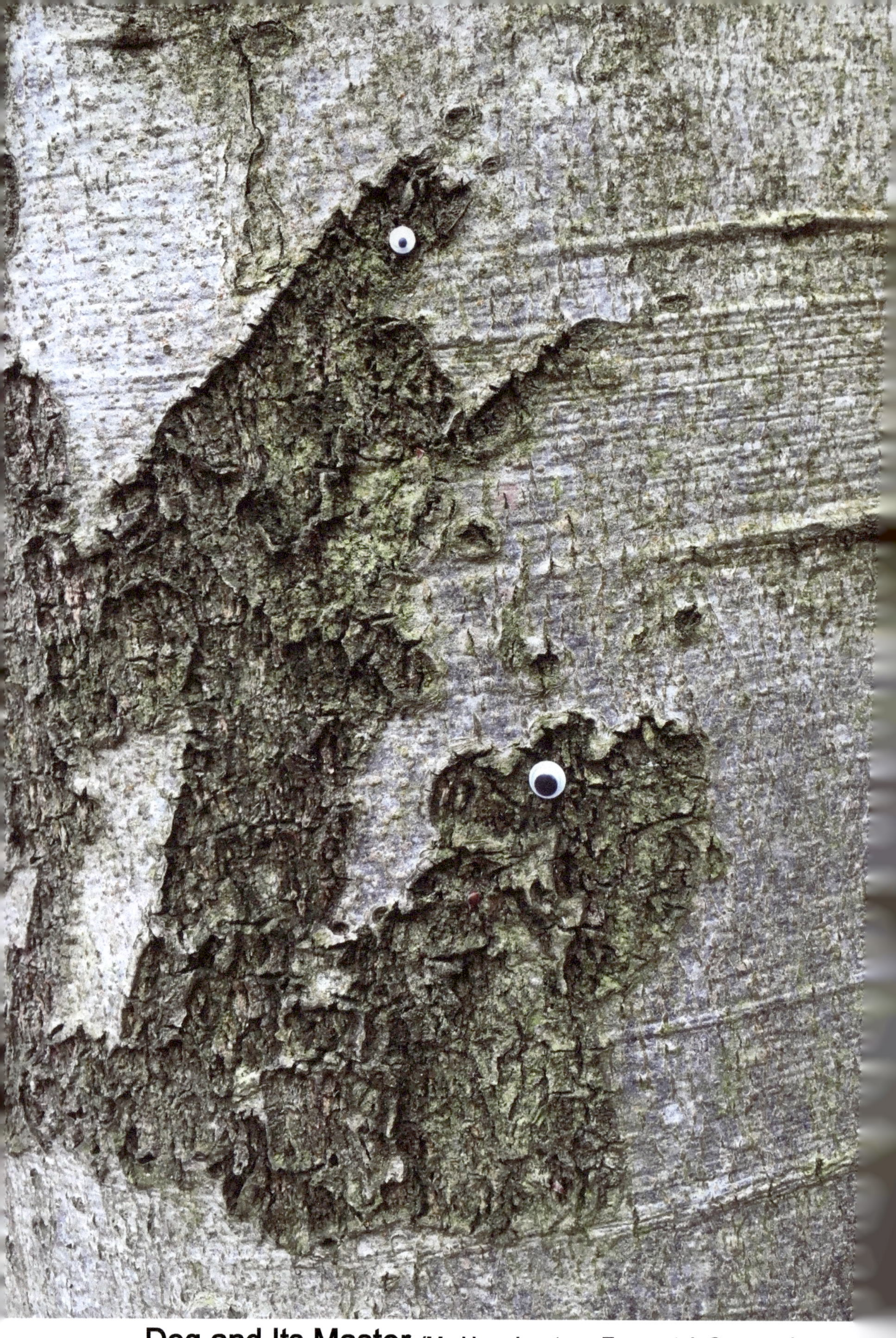

**Dog and Its Master** (Markings in a tree, Ennepetal, Germany)

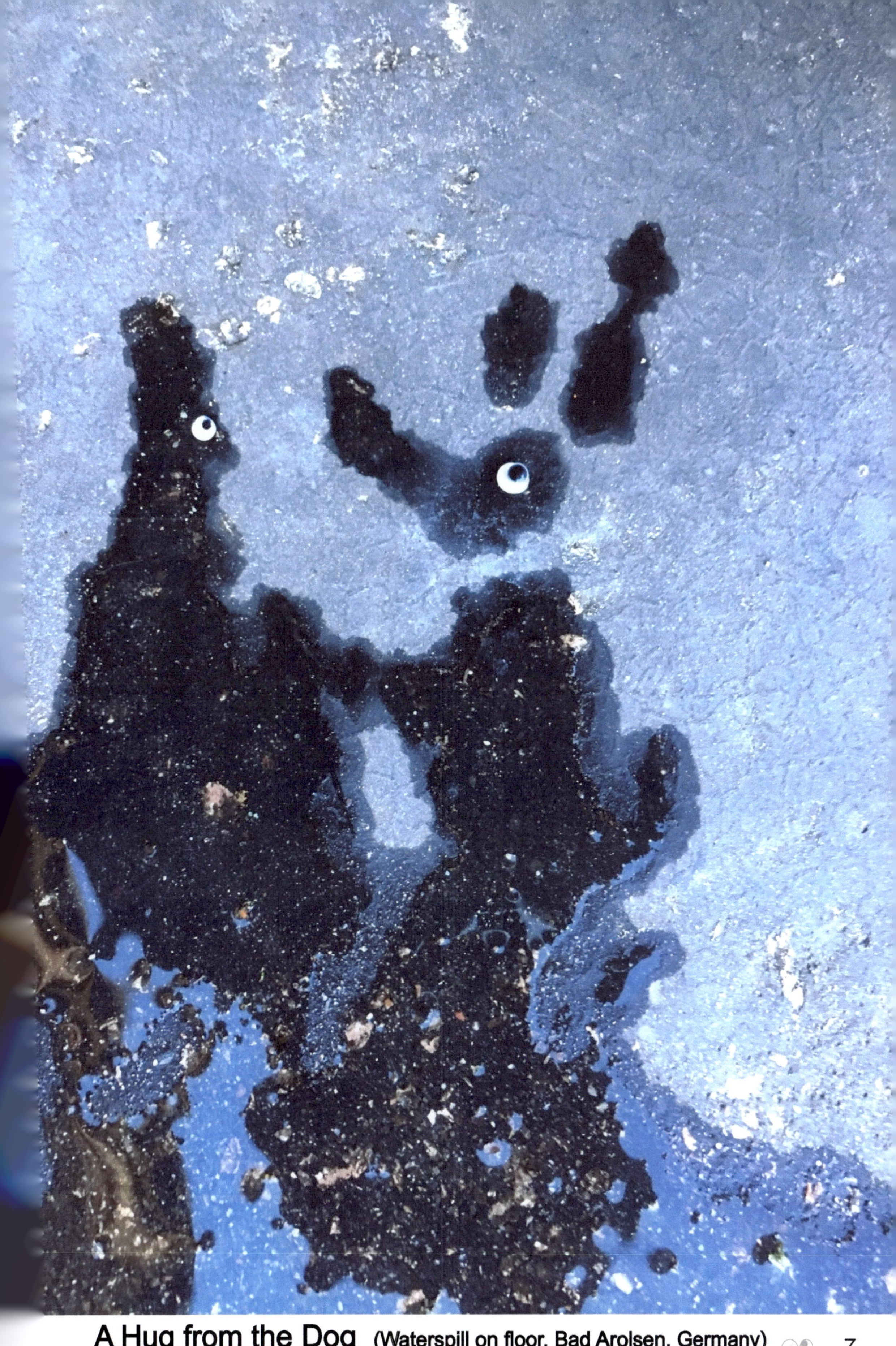

**A Hug from the Dog**  (Waterspill on floor, Bad Arolsen, Germany)  7

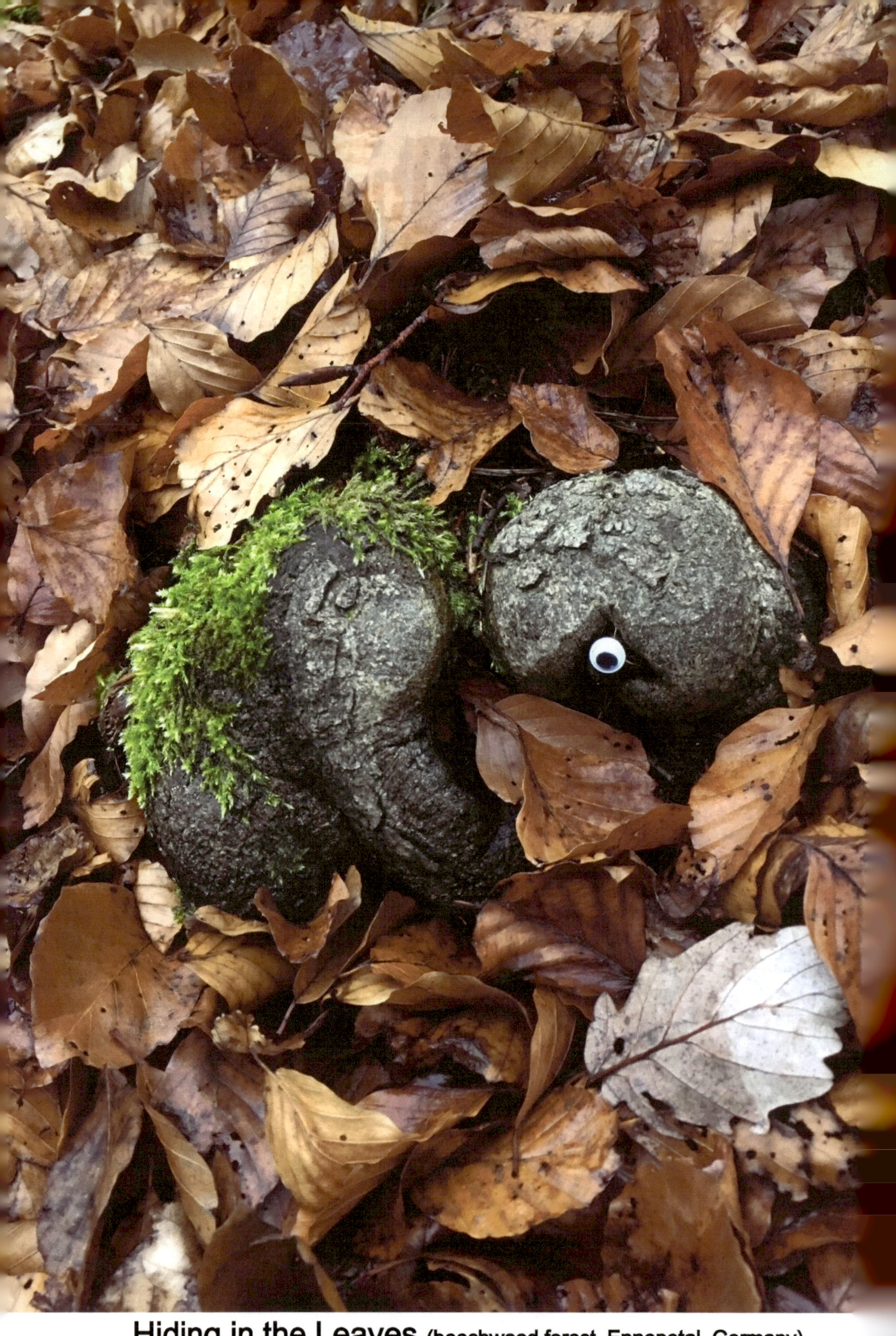

**Hiding in the Leaves** (beechwood forest, Ennepetal, Germany)

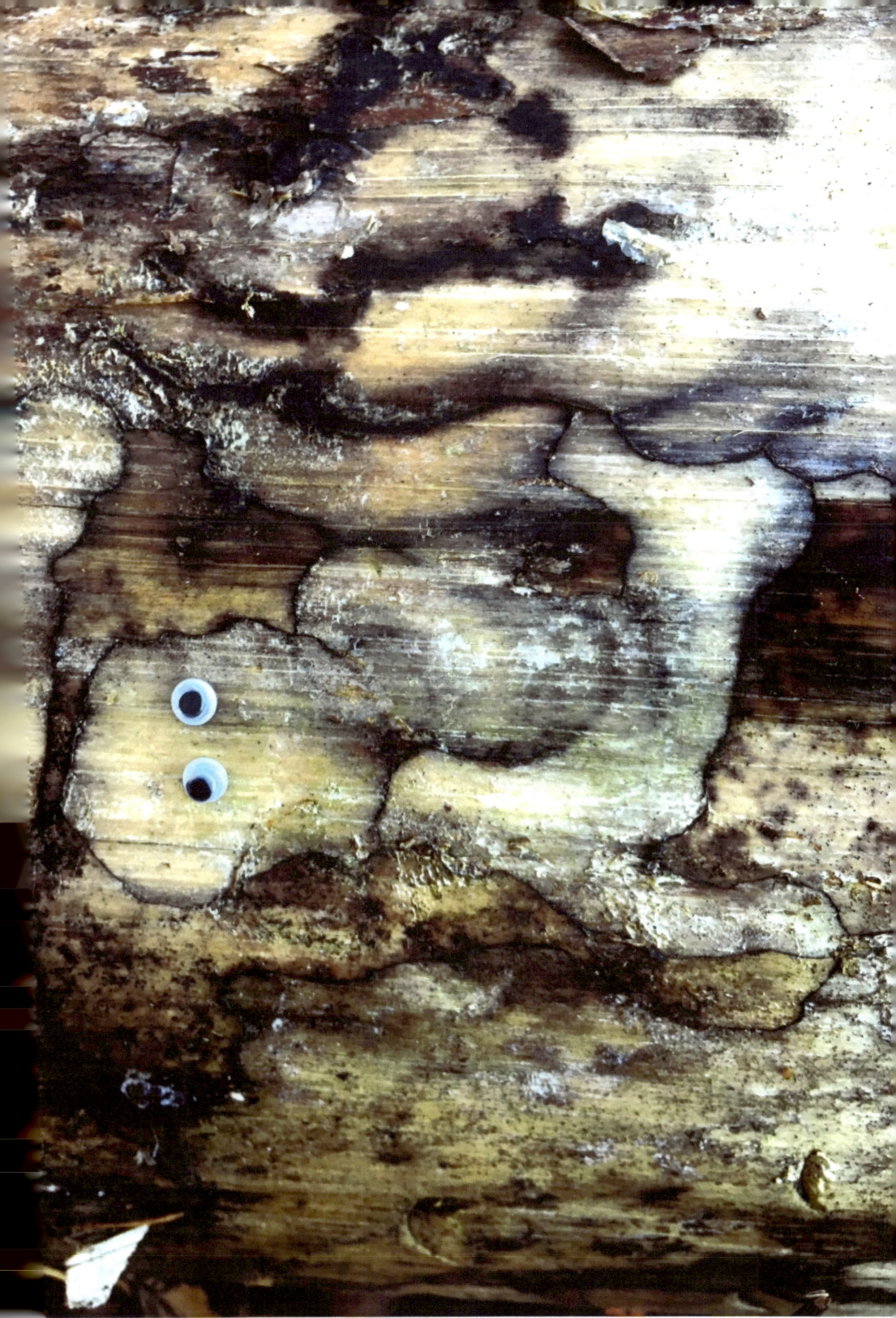

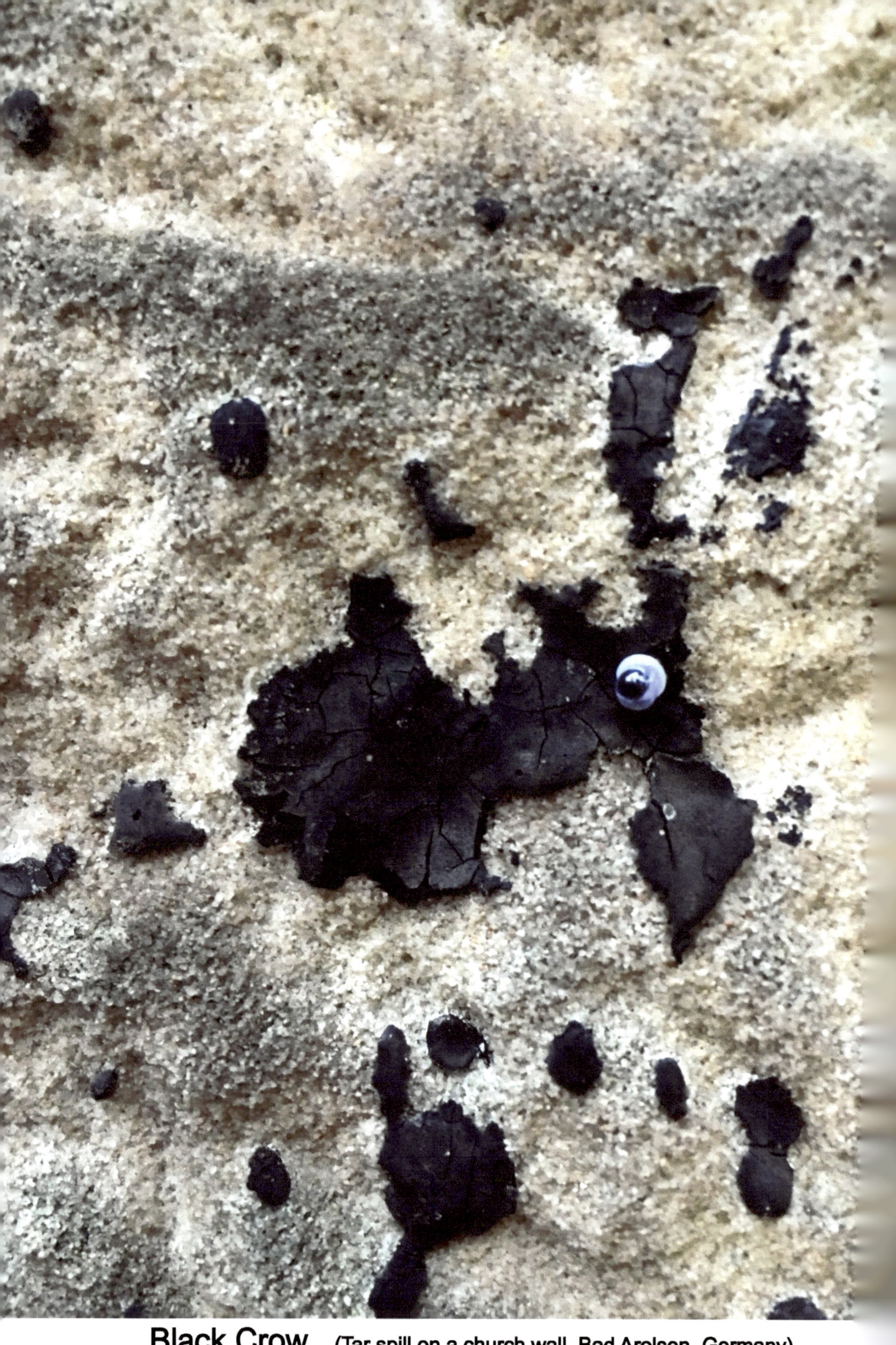

**Black Crow**   (Tar spill on a church wall, Bad Arolsen, Germany)

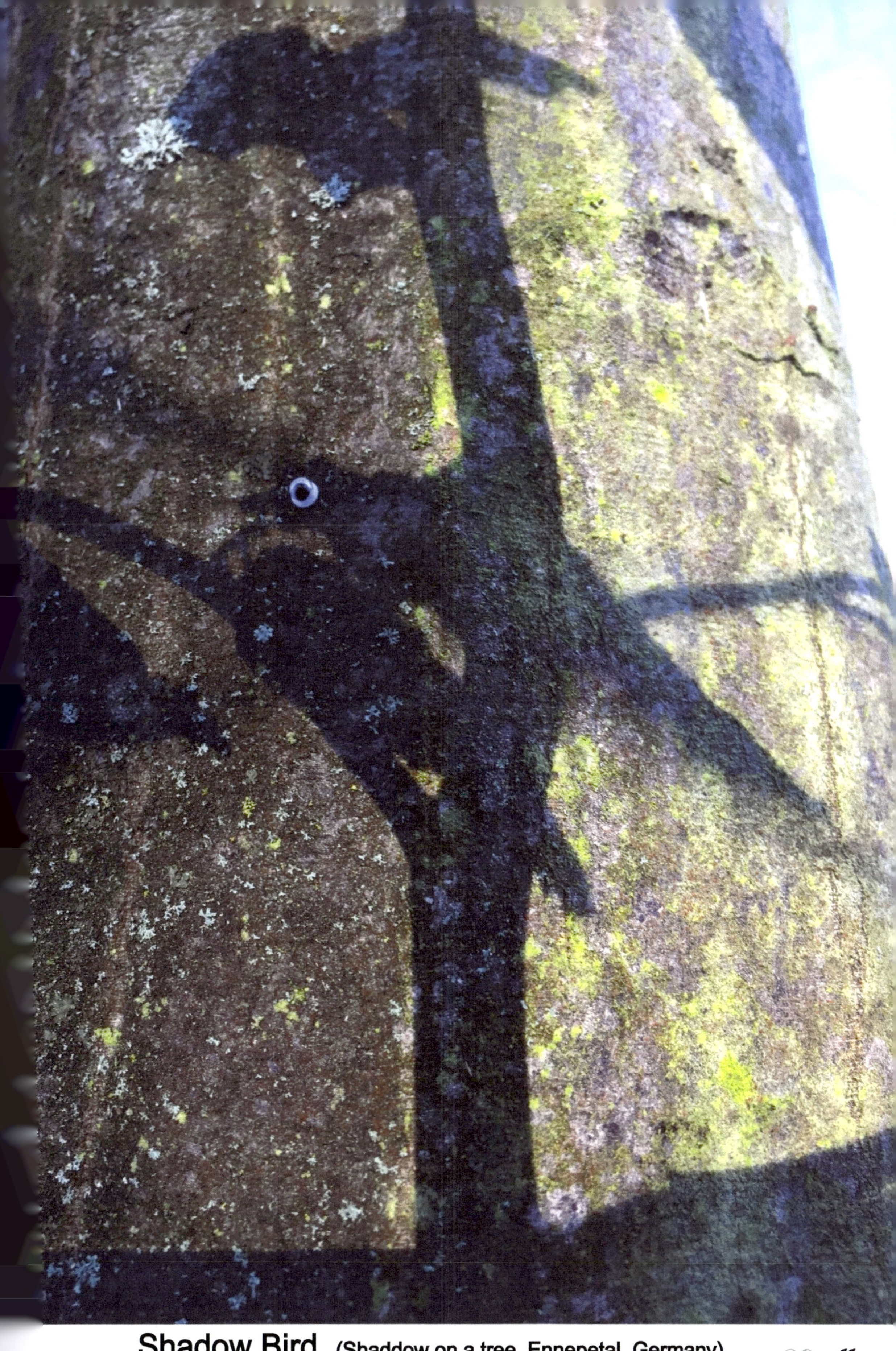

**Shadow Bird**  (Shaddow on a tree, Ennepetal, Germany)  11

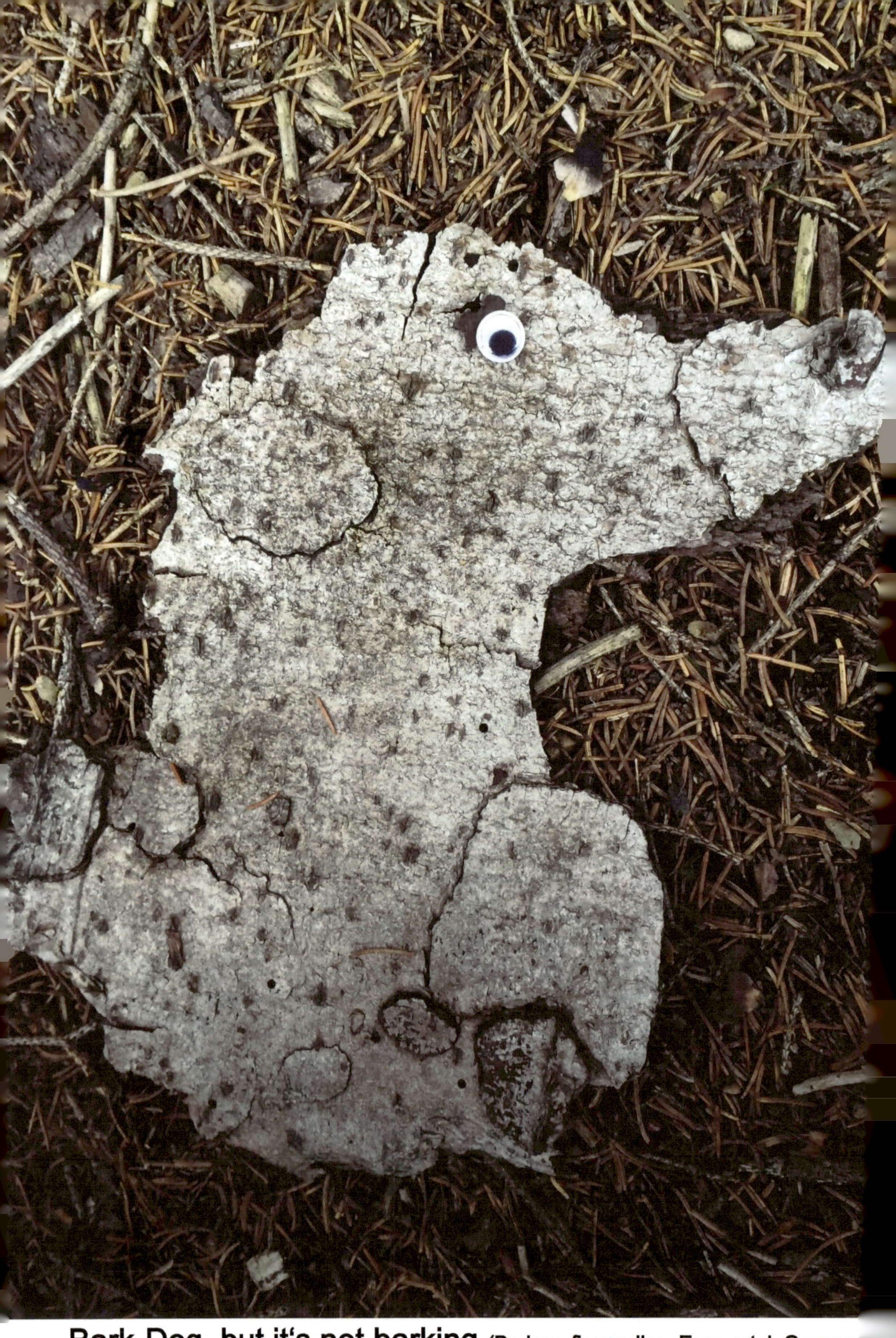

**Bark-Dog, but it's not barking** (Bark on fir needles, Ennepetal, German

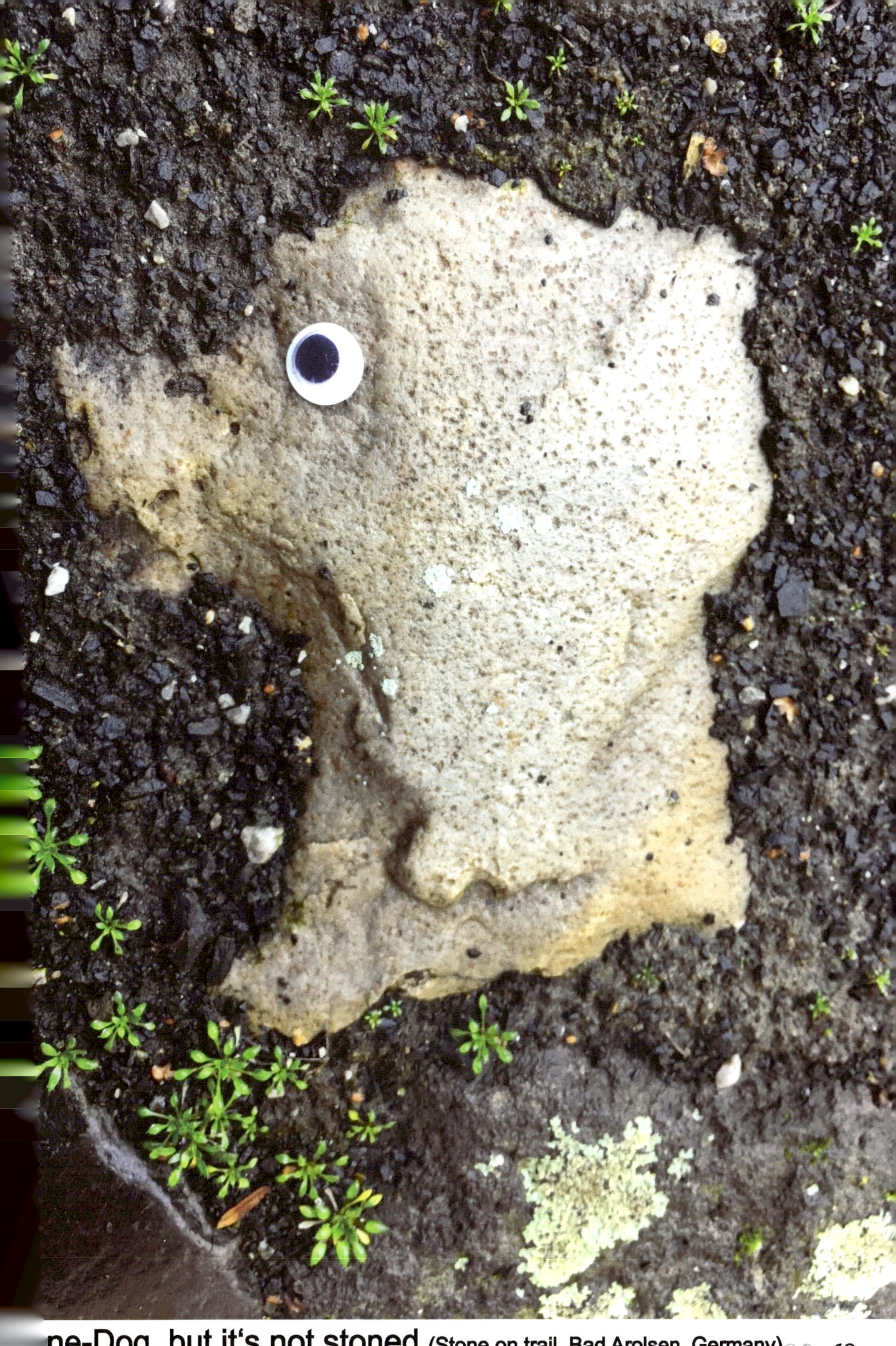

**ne-Dog, but it's not stoned** (Stone on trail, Bad Arolsen, Germany) 13

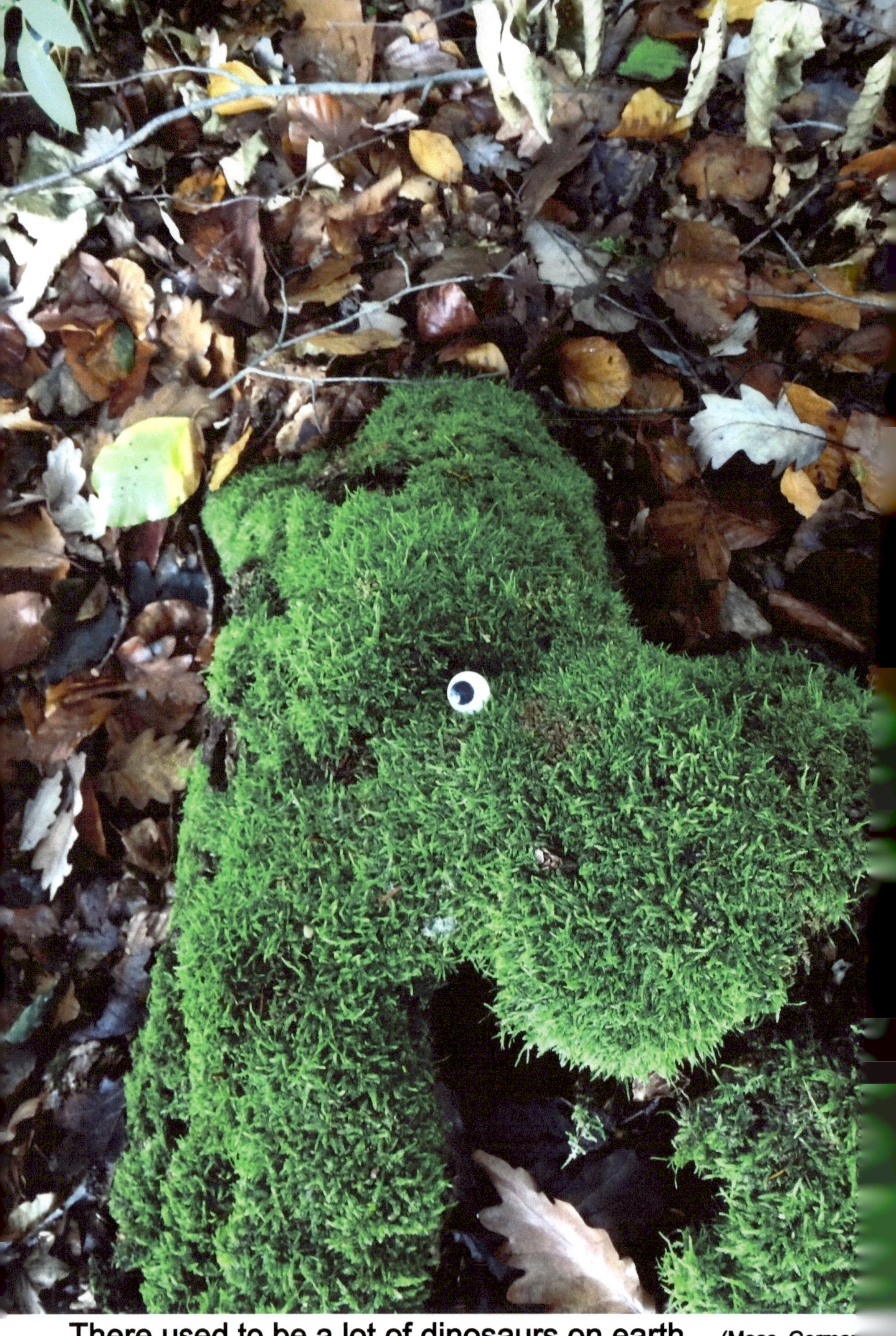

**There used to be a lot of dinosaurs on earth…** (Moss, Germar

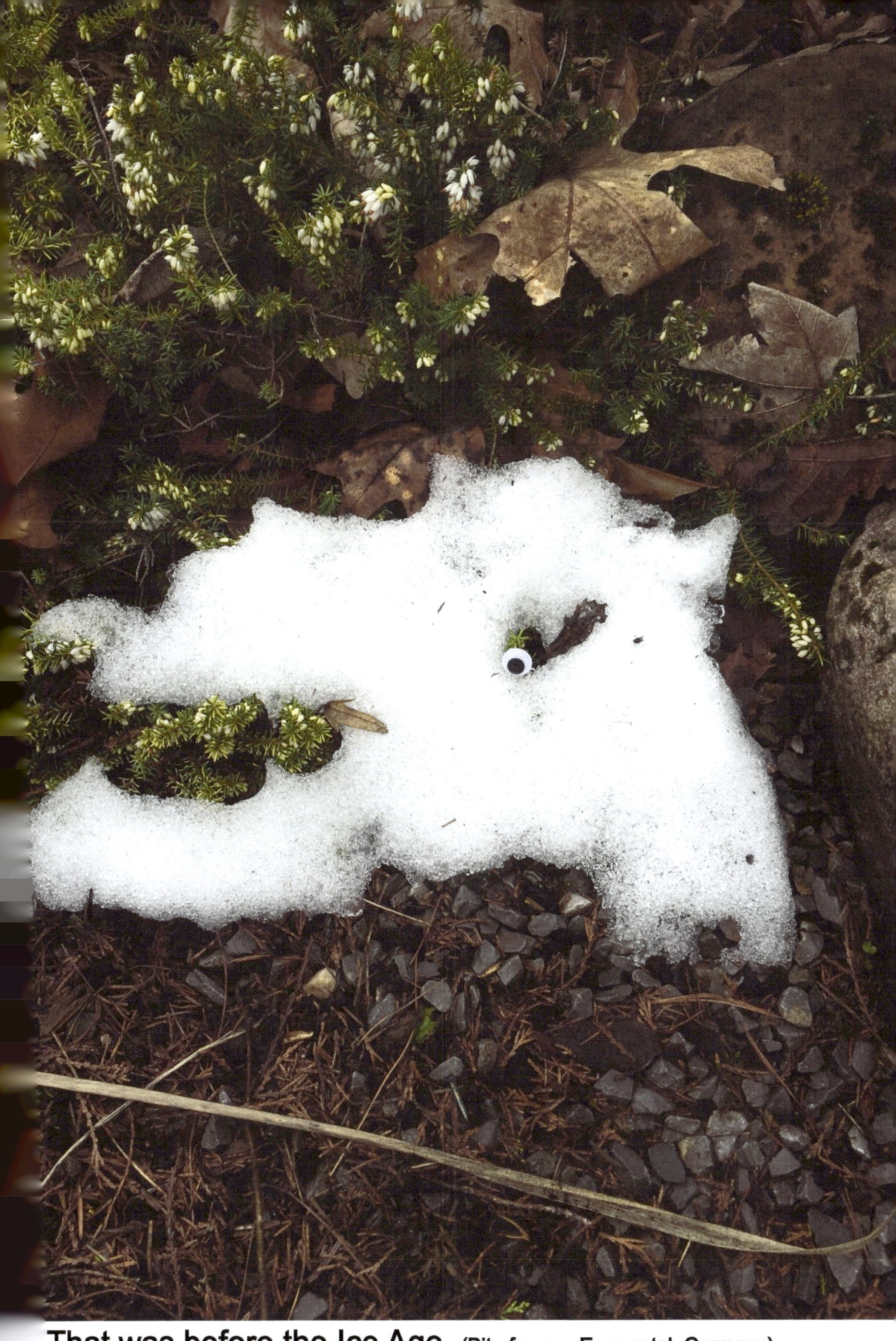

**That was before the Ice Age.** (Bit of snow, Ennepetal, Germany)  15

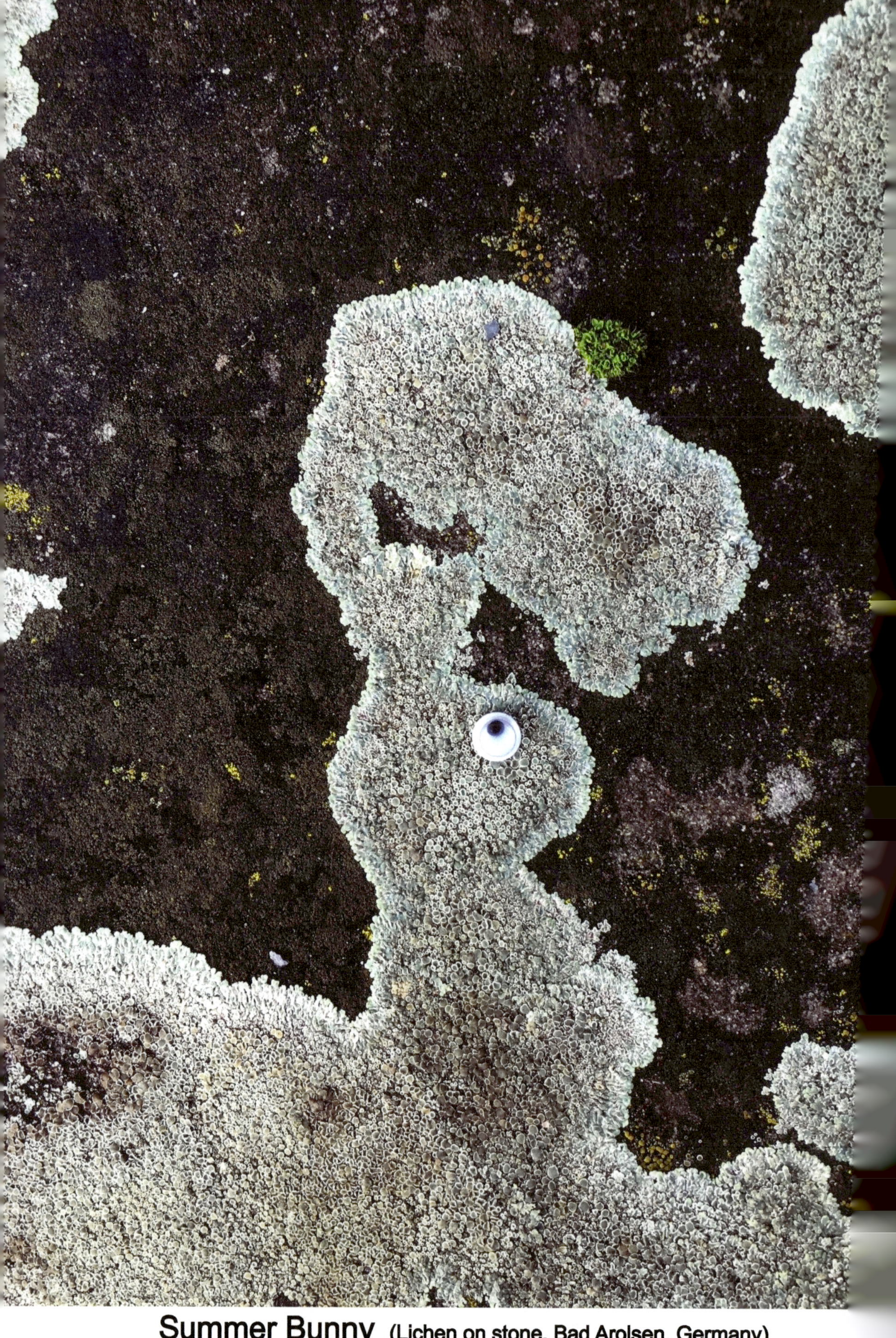

**Summer Bunny** (Lichen on stone, Bad Arolsen, Germany)

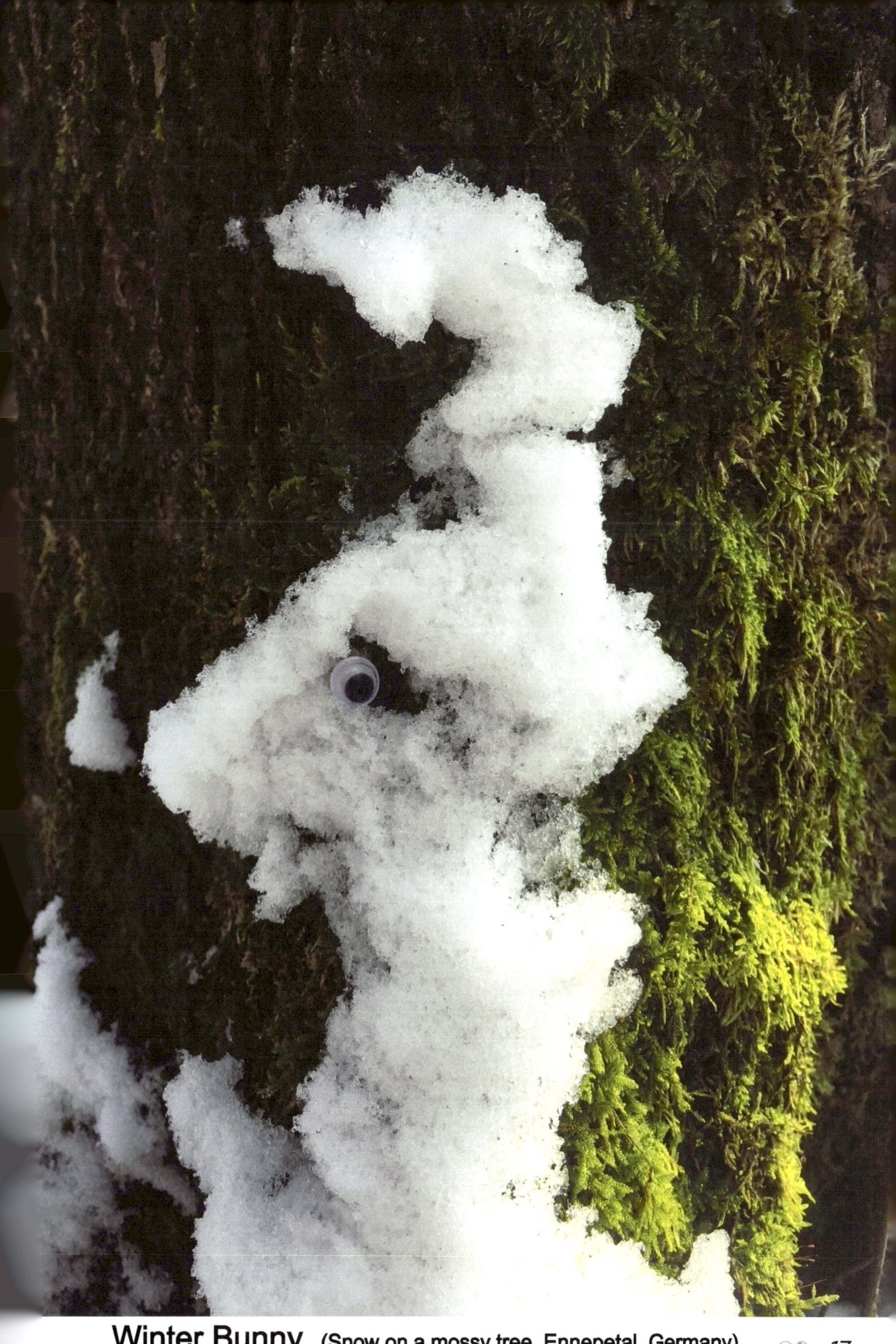

**Winter Bunny** (Snow on a mossy tree, Ennepetal, Germany)

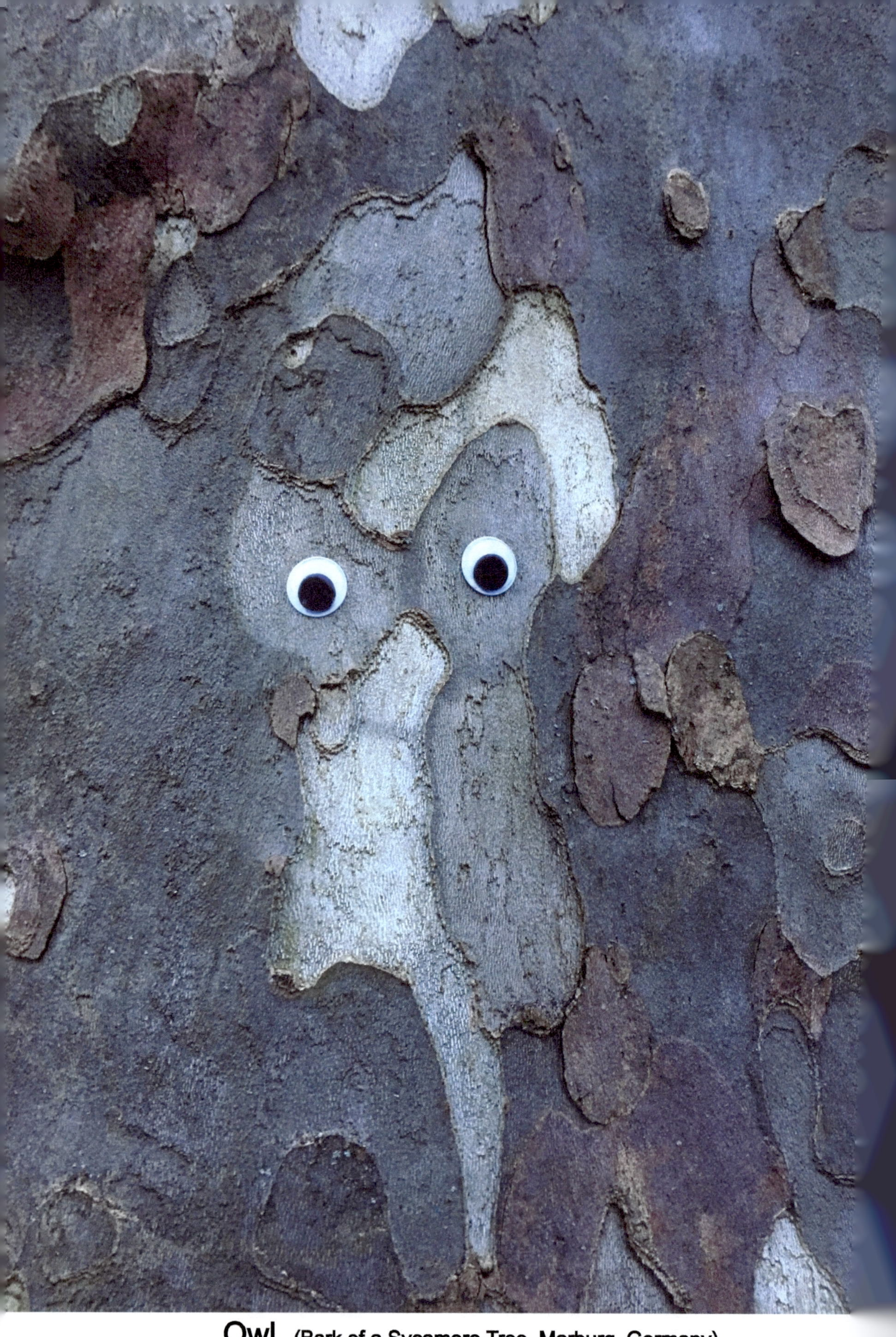

Owl  (Bark of a Sycamore Tree, Marburg, Germany)

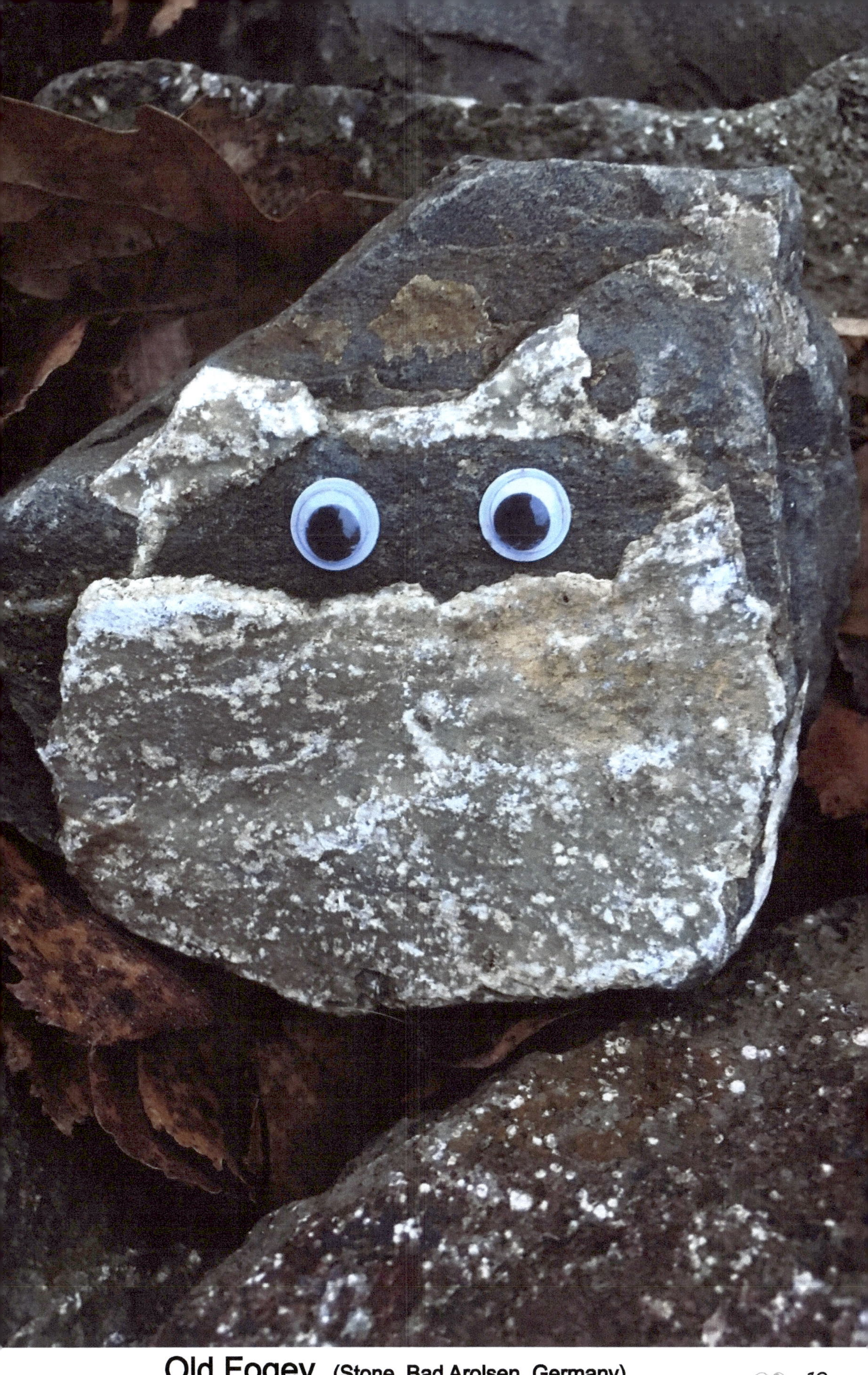

**Old Fogey**  (Stone, Bad Arolsen, Germany)

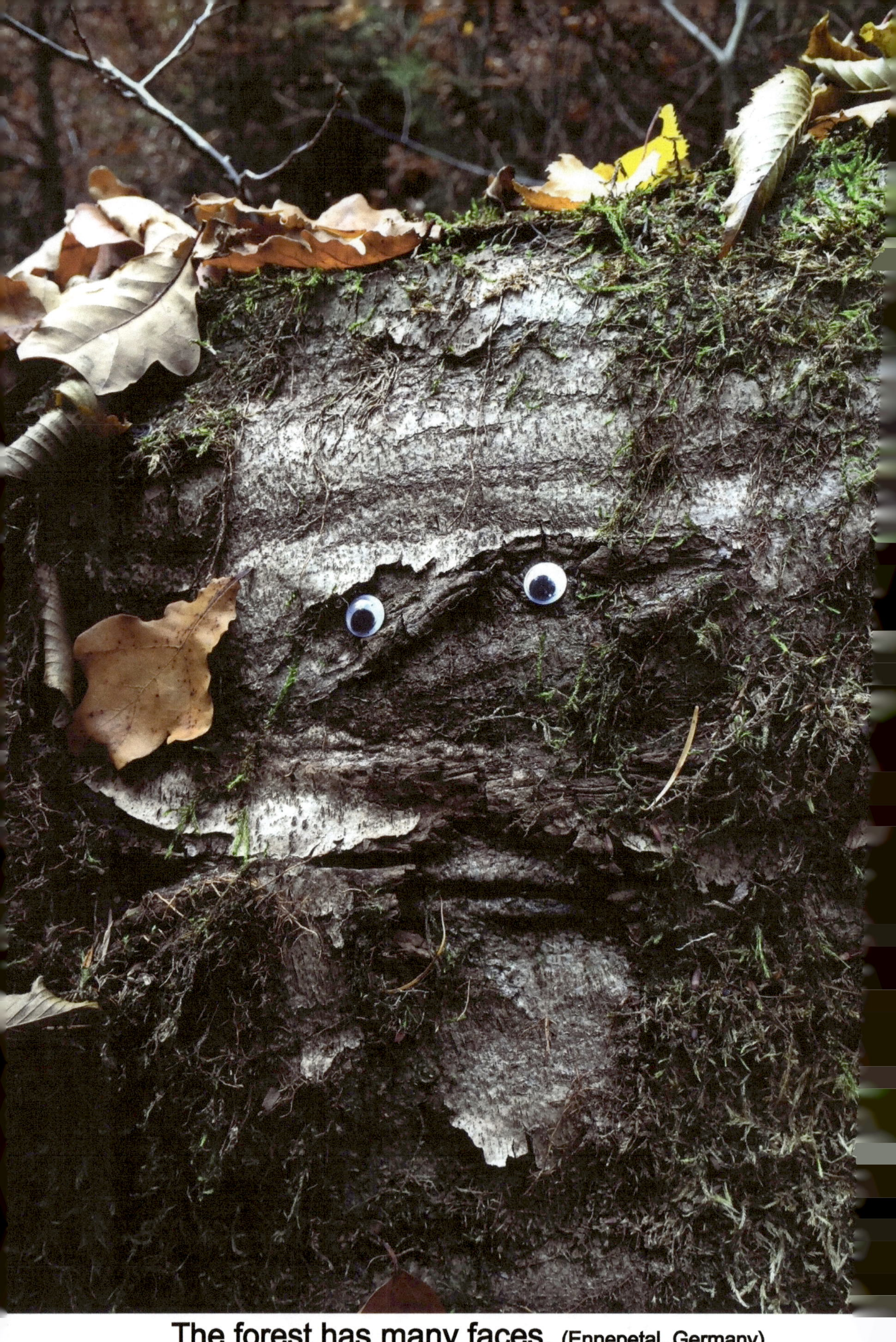

**The forest has many faces.** (Ennepetal, Germany)

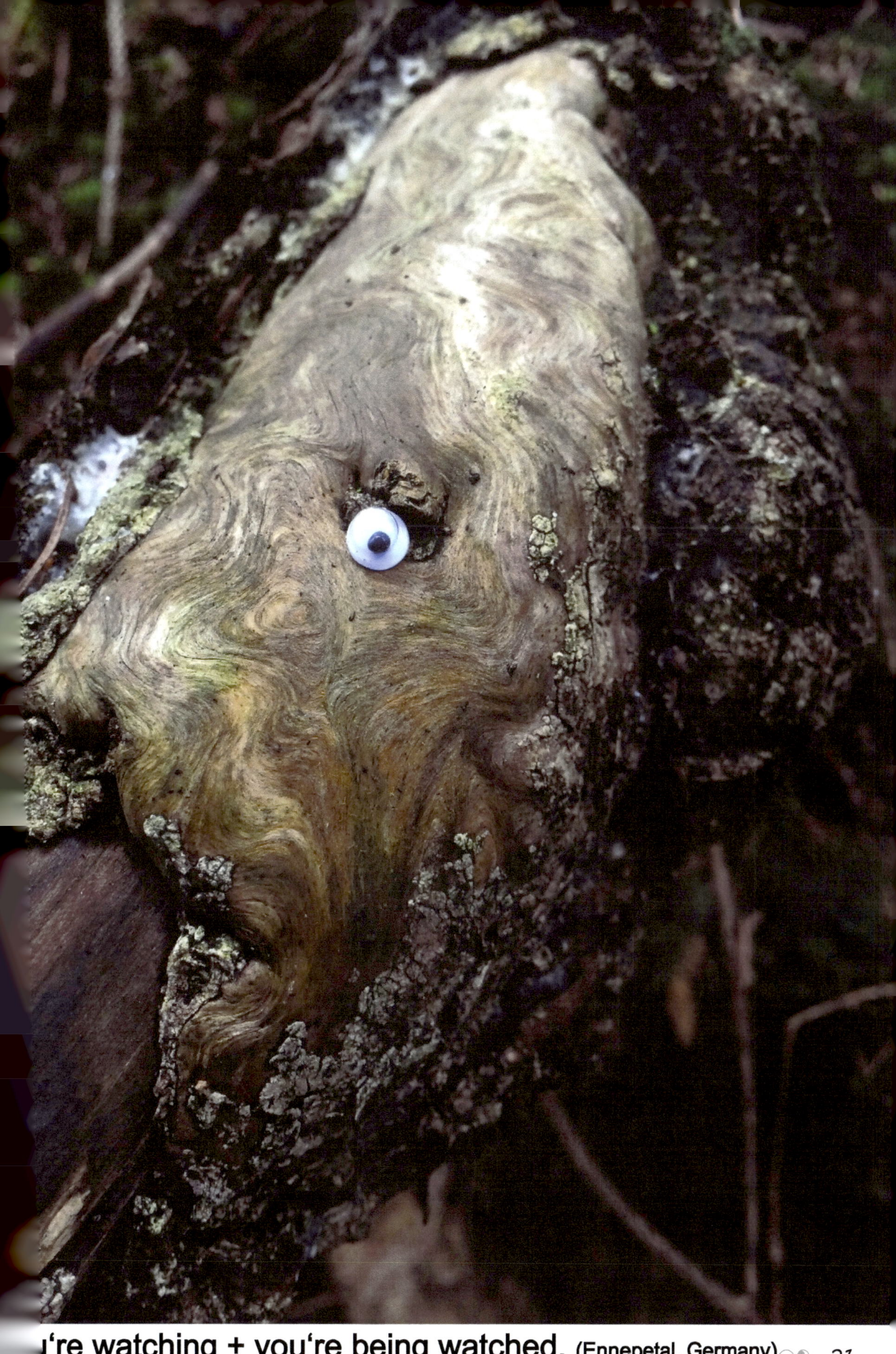

u're watching + you're being watched. (Ennepetal, Germany)

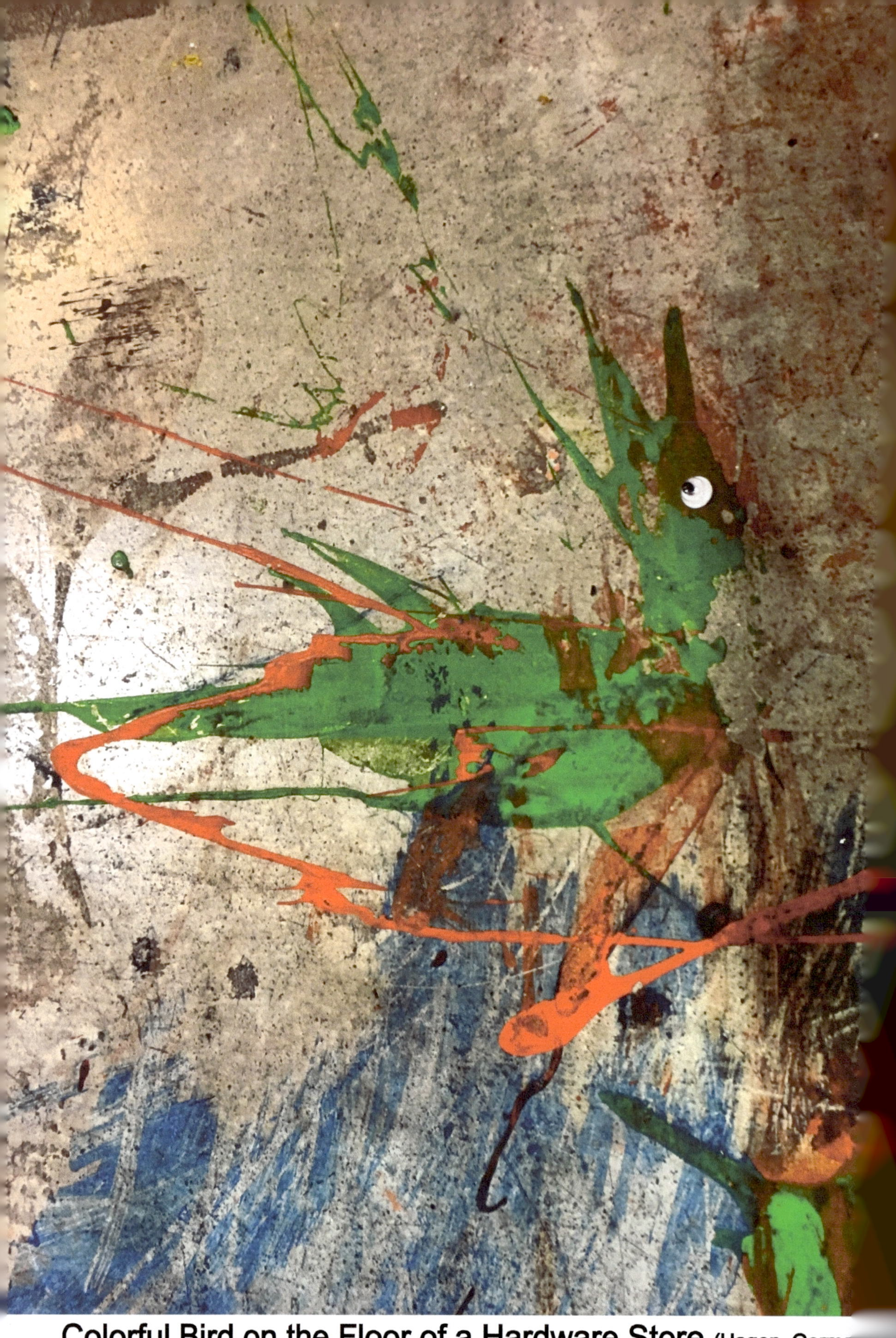

**Colorful Bird on the Floor of a Hardware Store** (Hagen, Germa

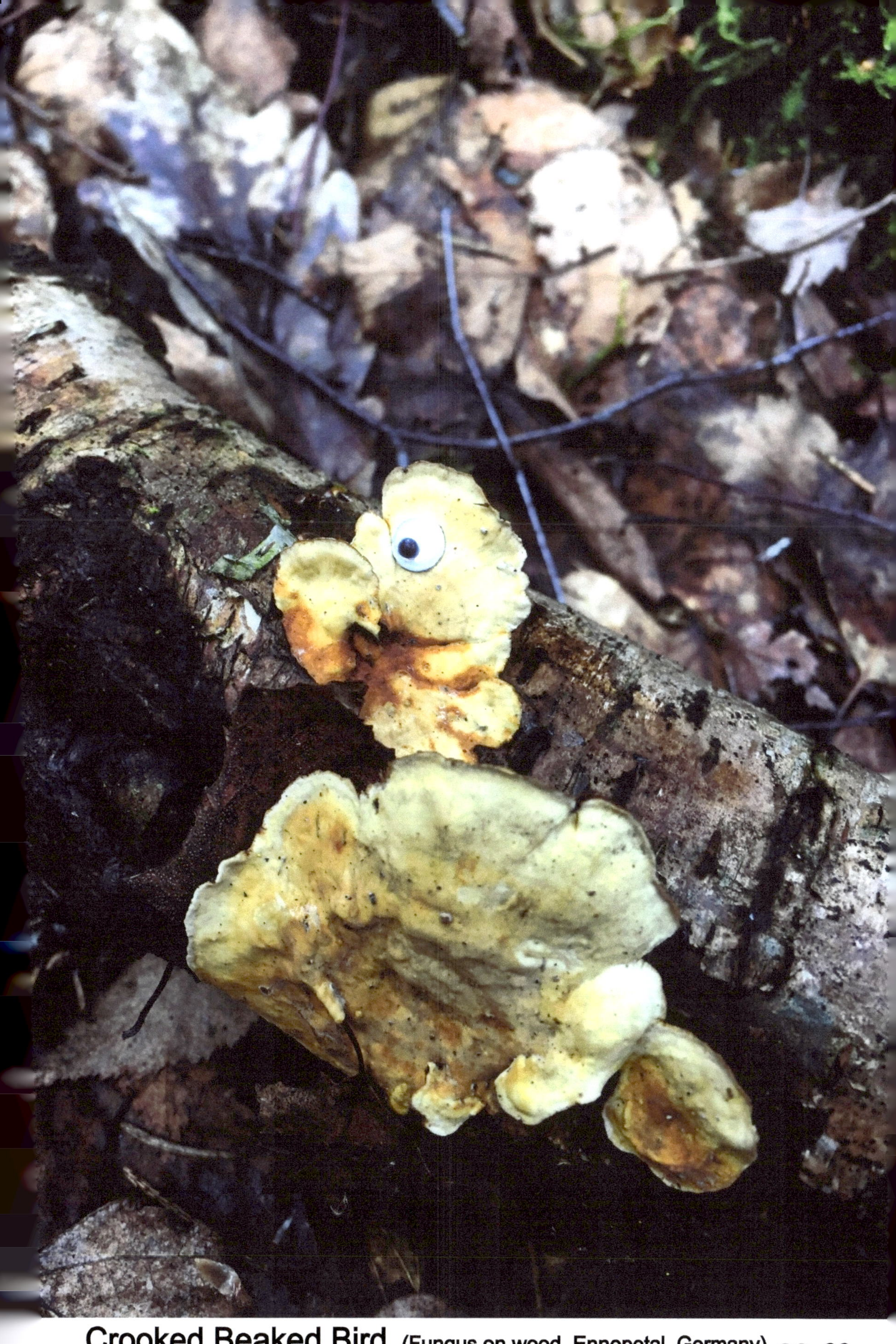

**Crooked Beaked Bird**  (Fungus on wood, Ennepetal, Germany)  23

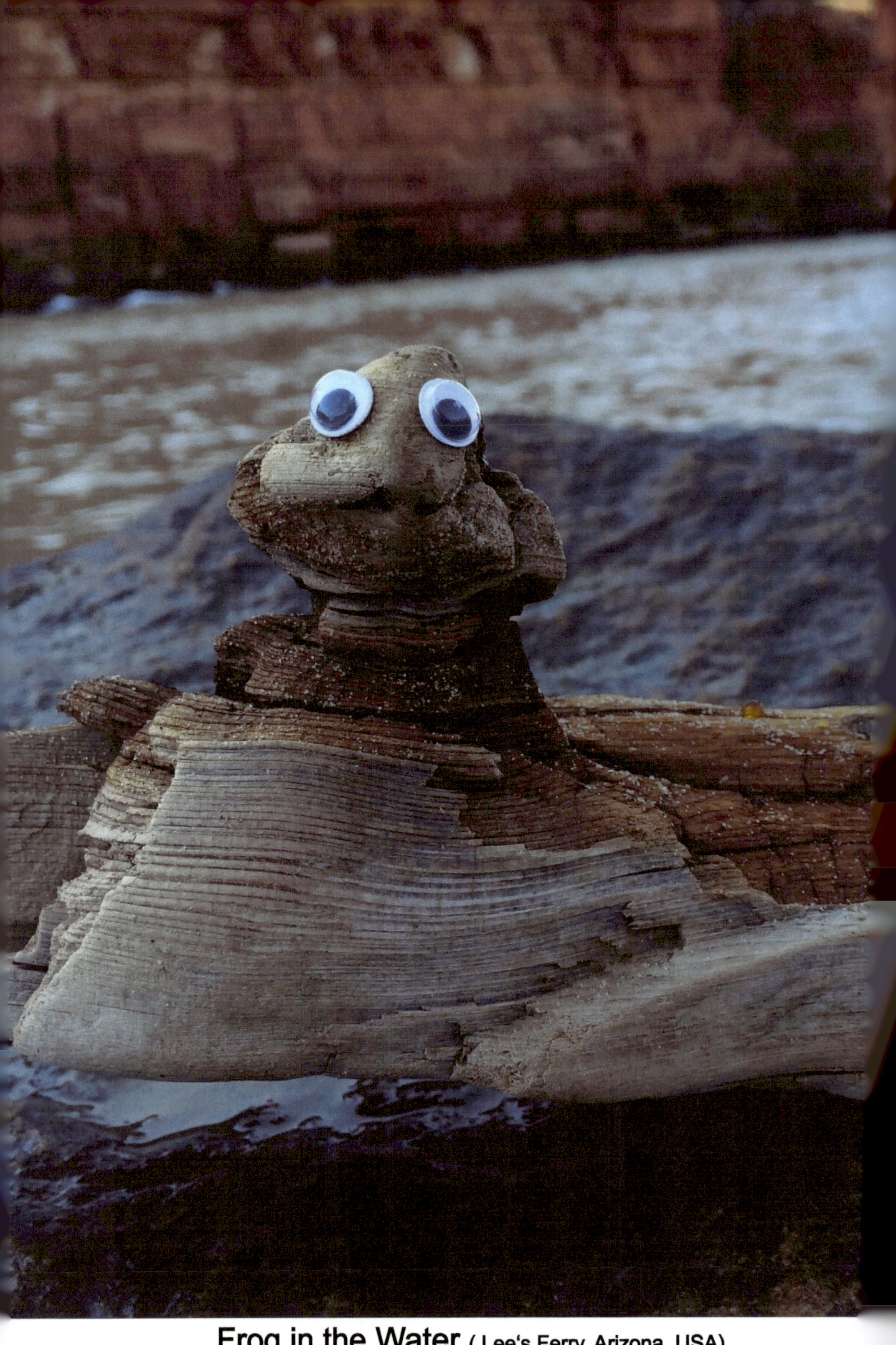

**Frog in the Water** ( Lee's Ferry, Arizona, USA)

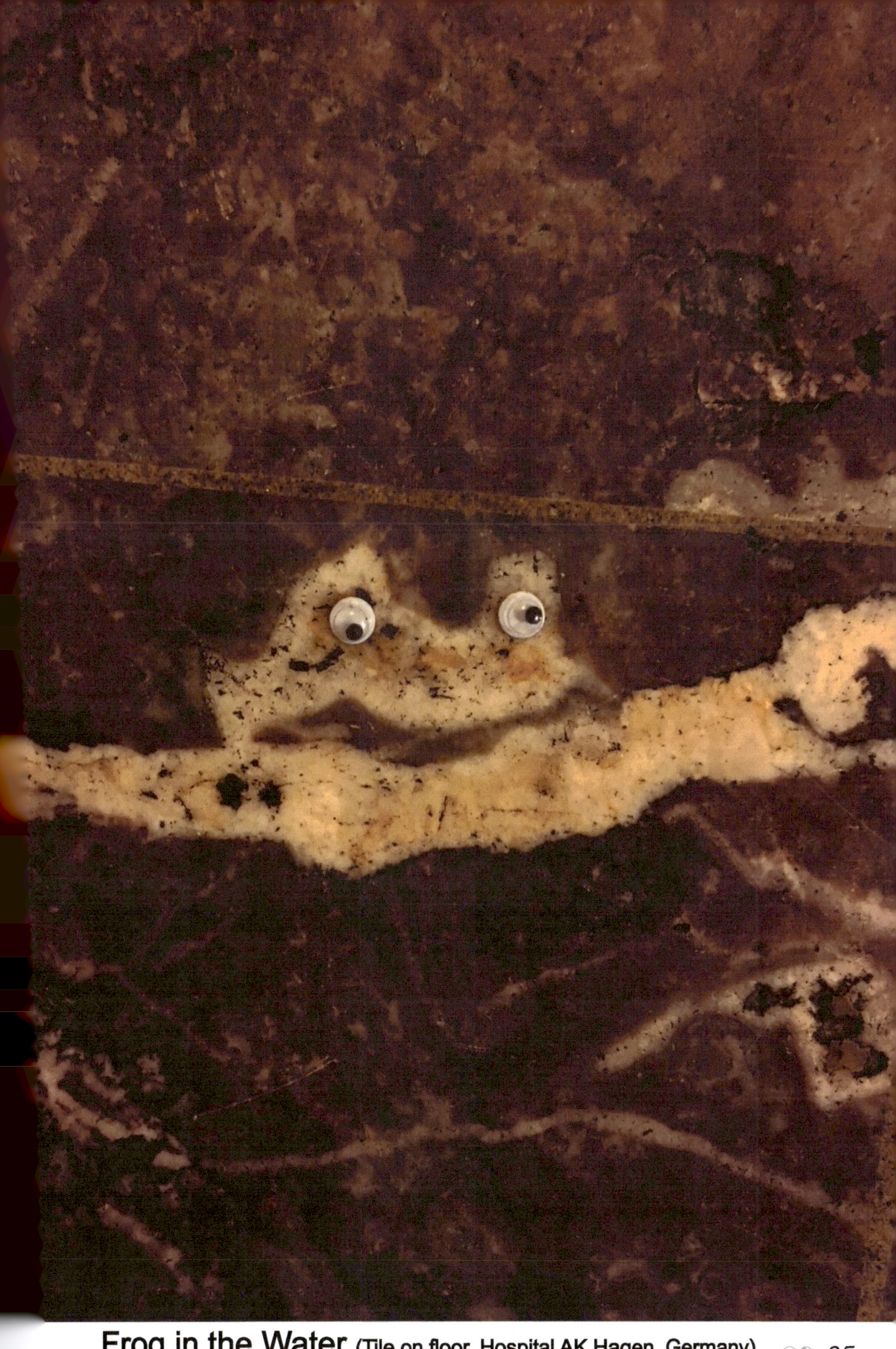

**Frog in the Water** (Tile on floor, Hospital AK Hagen, Germany) 25

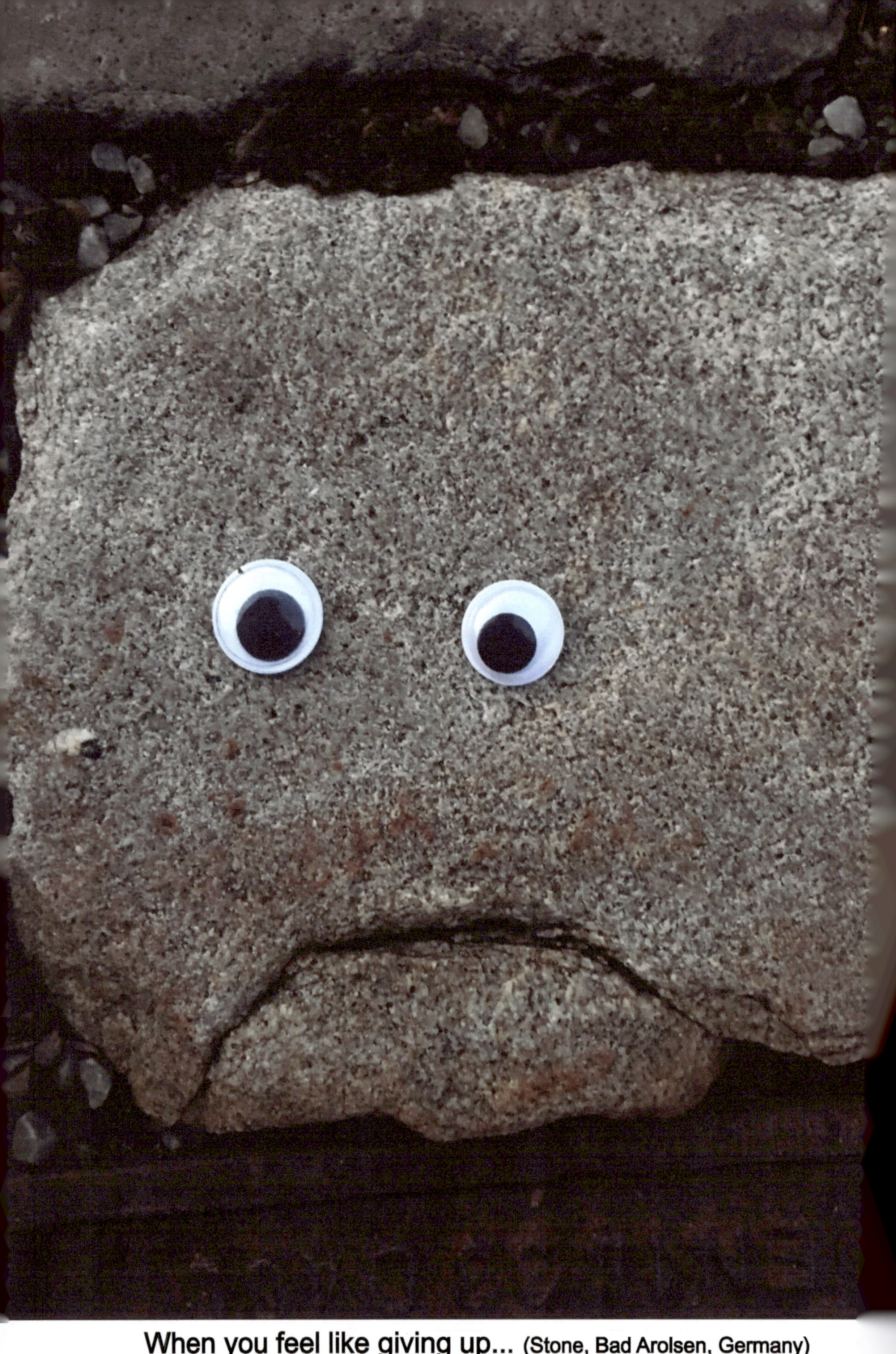

When you feel like giving up… (Stone, Bad Arolsen, Germany)

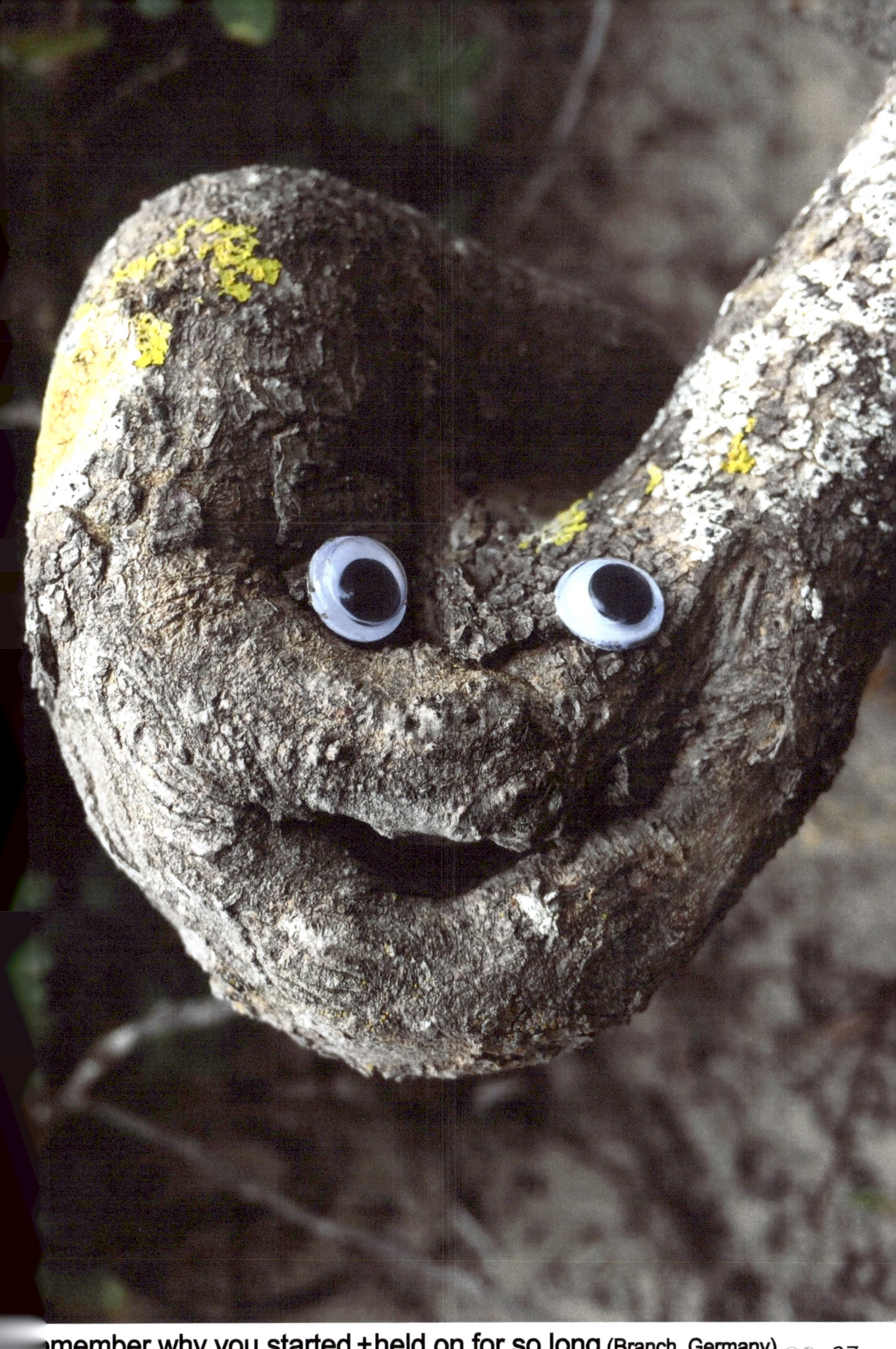

emember why you started +held on for so long (Branch, Germany) 👀 27

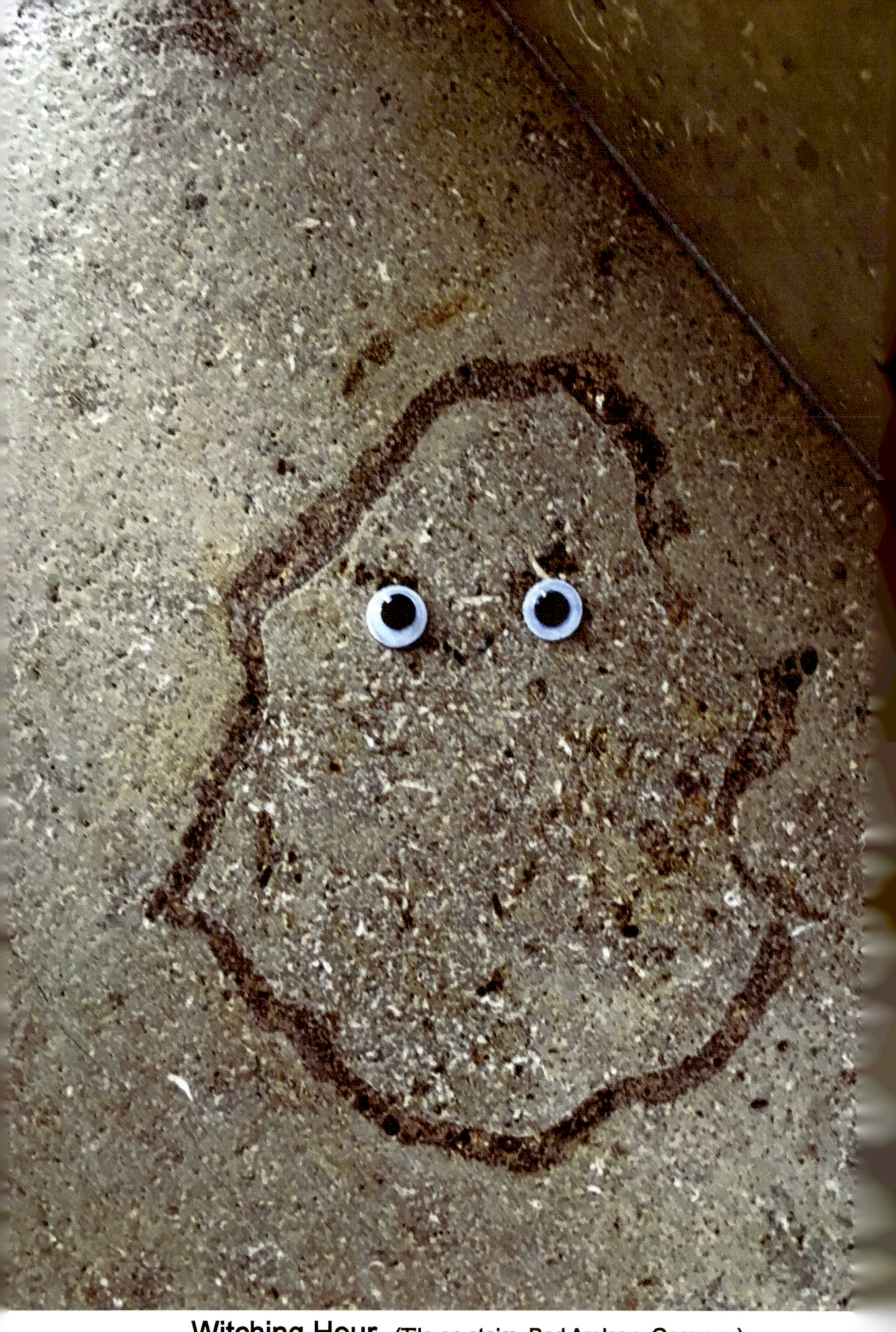

**Witching Hour** (Tile on stairs, Bad Arolsen, Germany)

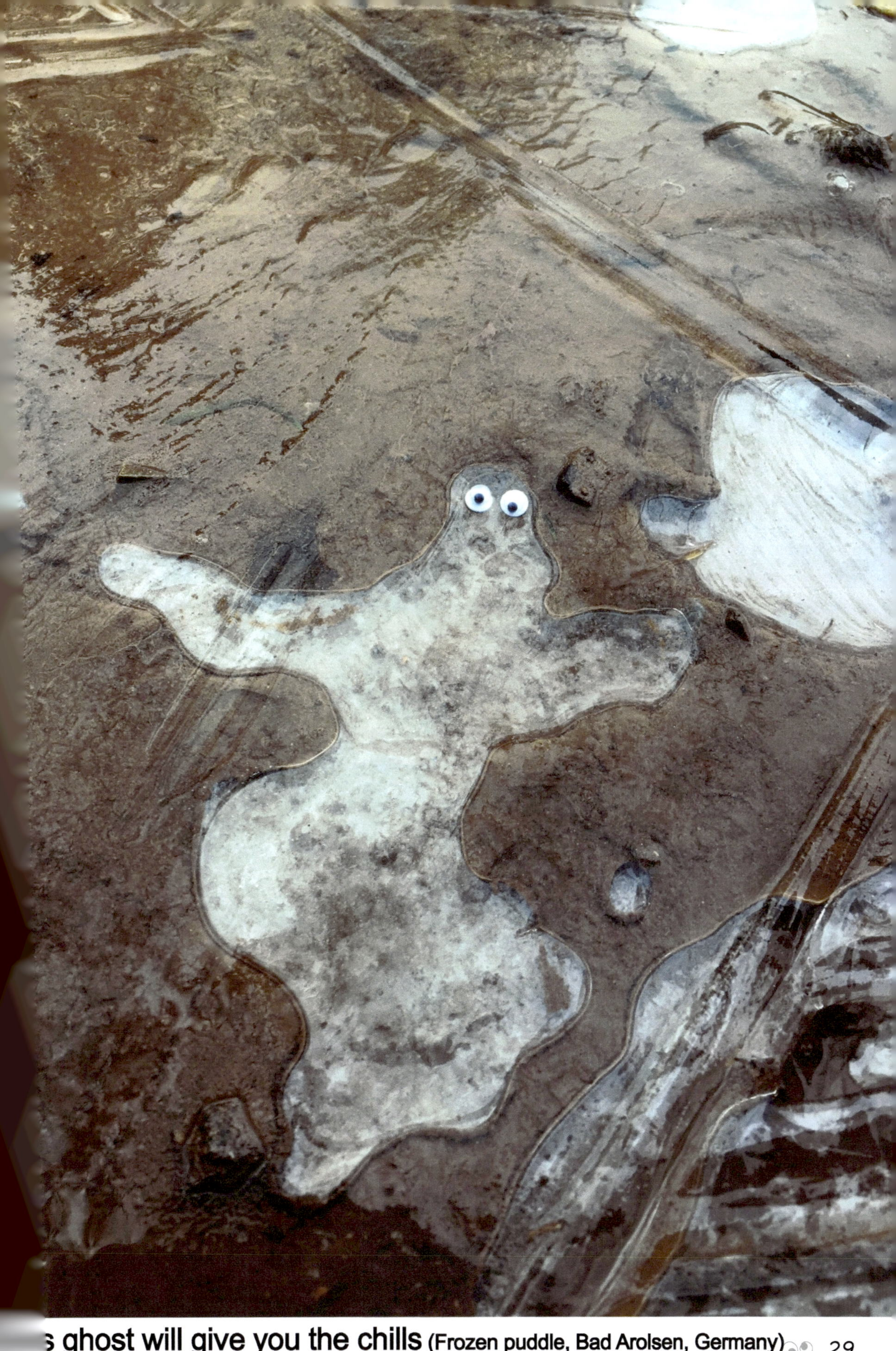

s ghost will give you the chills (Frozen puddle, Bad Arolsen, Germany) 29

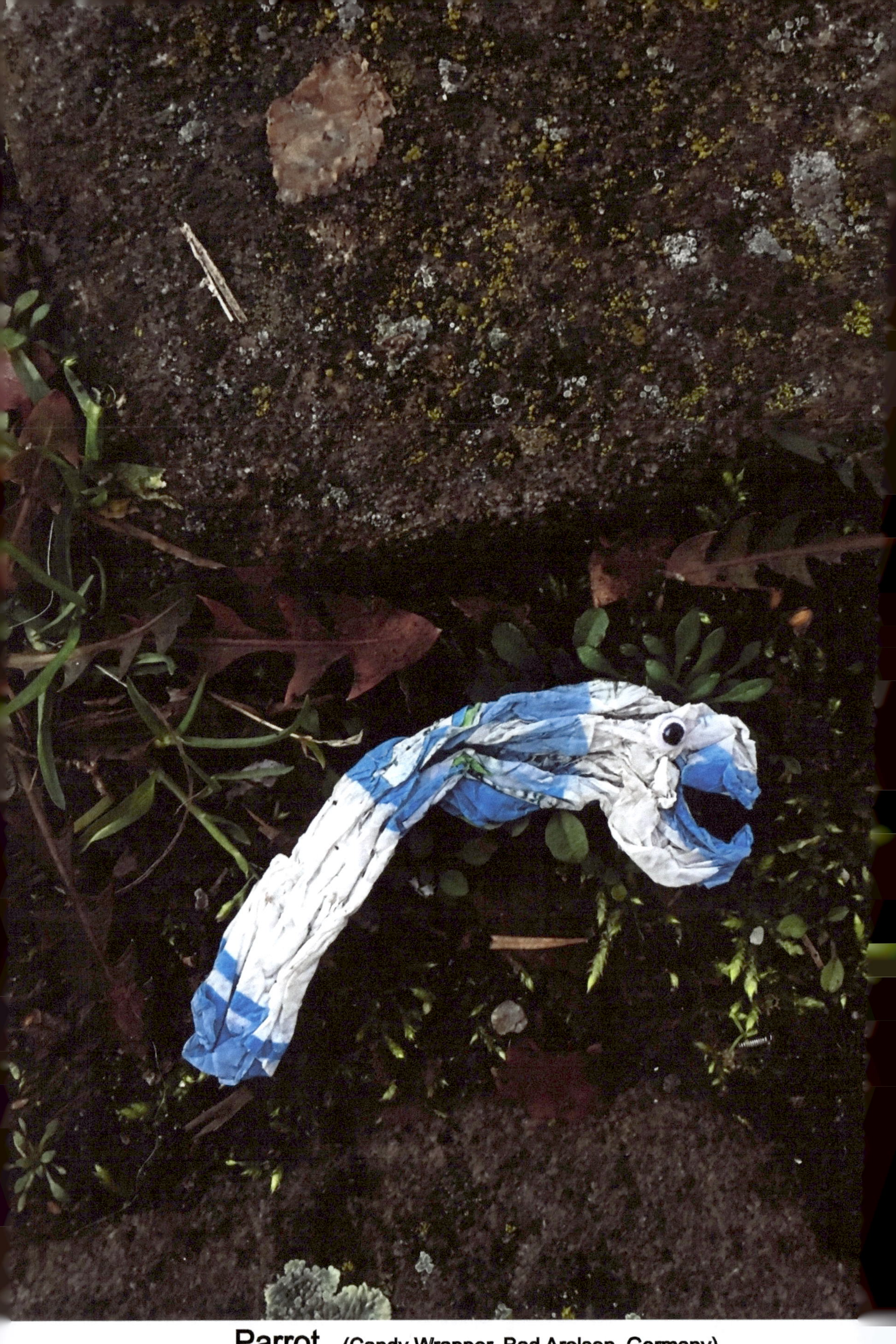

**Parrot**   (Candy Wrapper, Bad Arolsen, Germany)

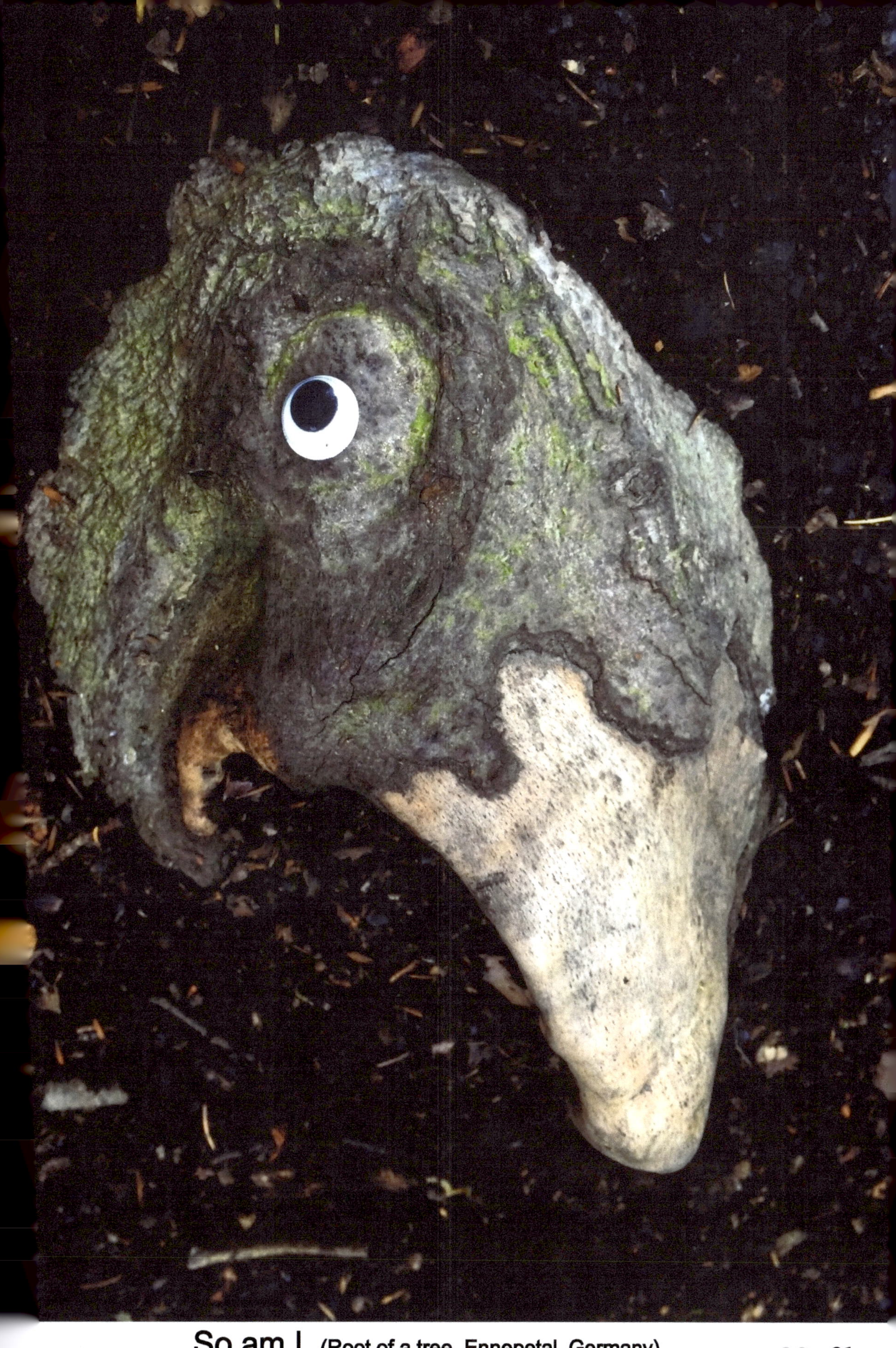

**So am I**  (Root of a tree, Ennepetal, Germany)

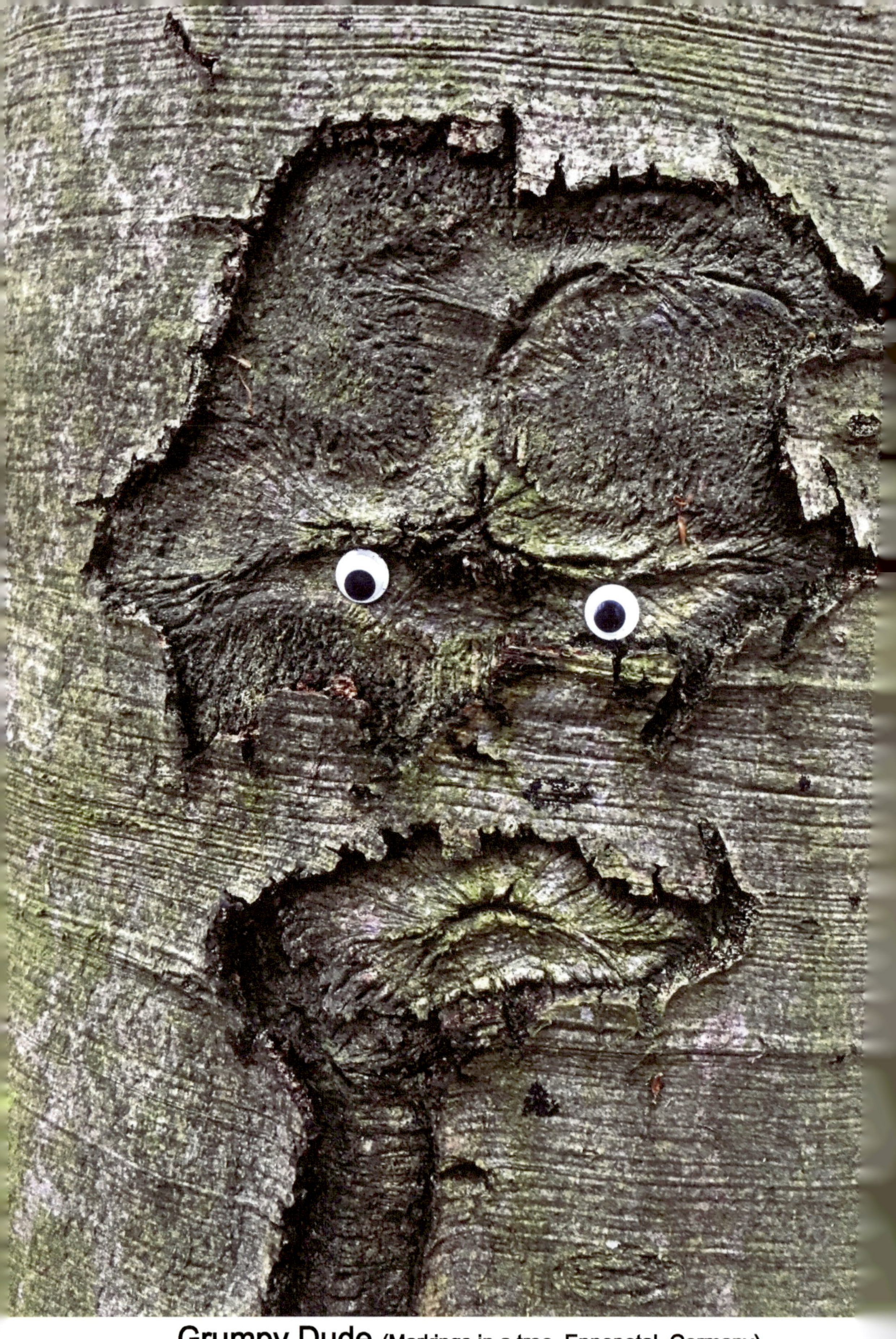

**Grumpy Dude** (Markings in a tree, Ennepetal, Germany)

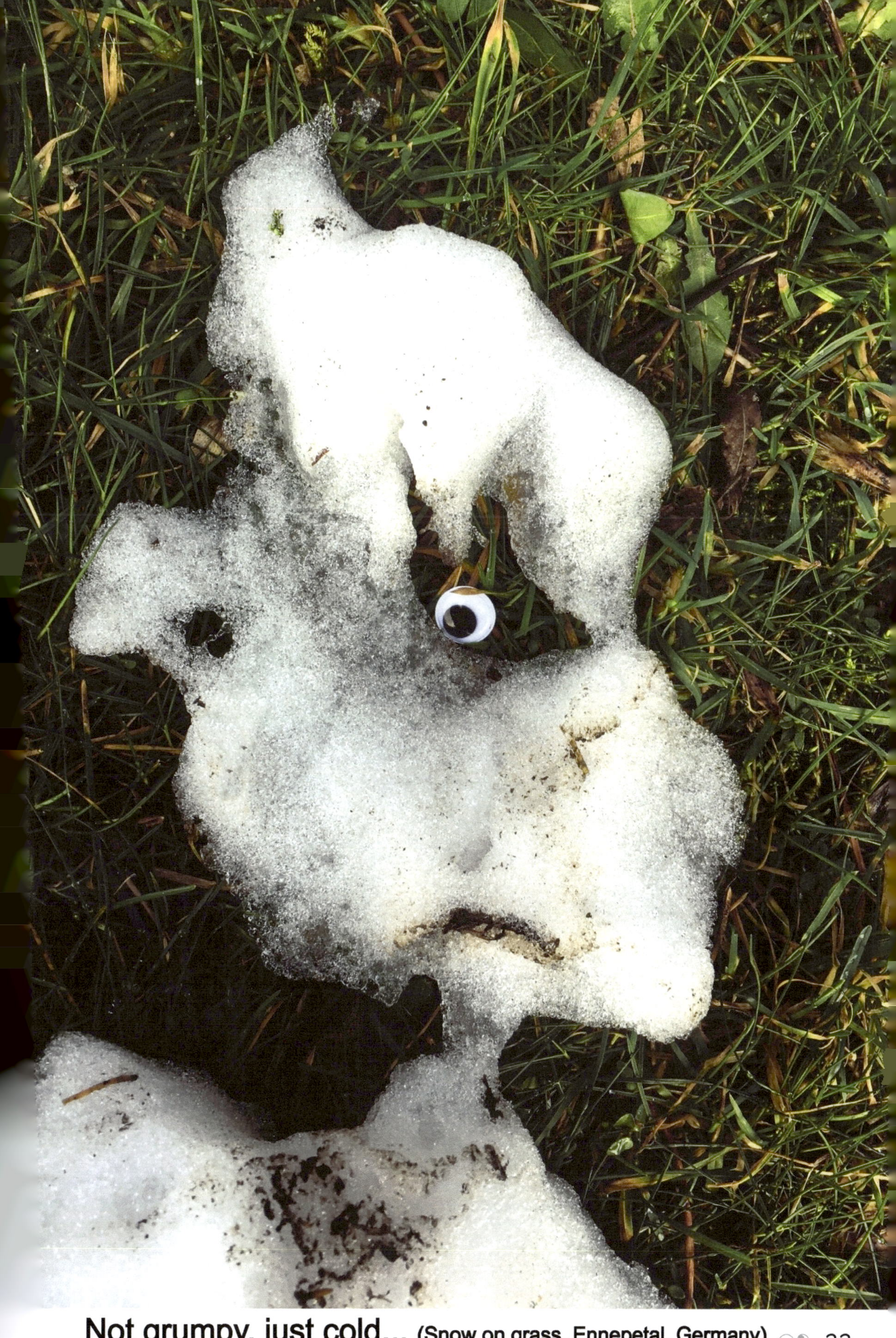

**Not grumpy, just cold…** (Snow on grass, Ennepetal, Germany) 33

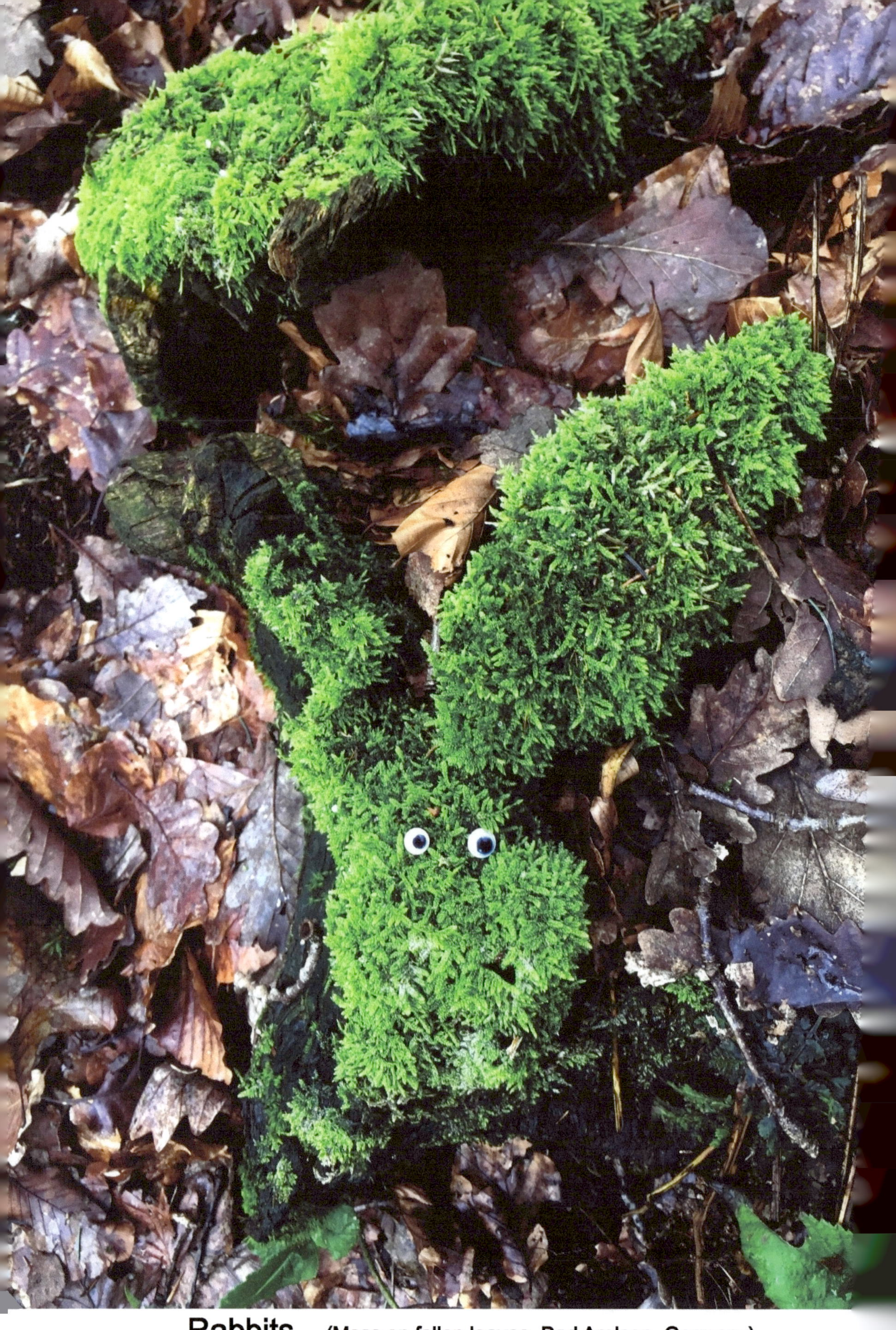

**Rabbits...** (Moss on fallen leaves, Bad Arolsen, Germany)

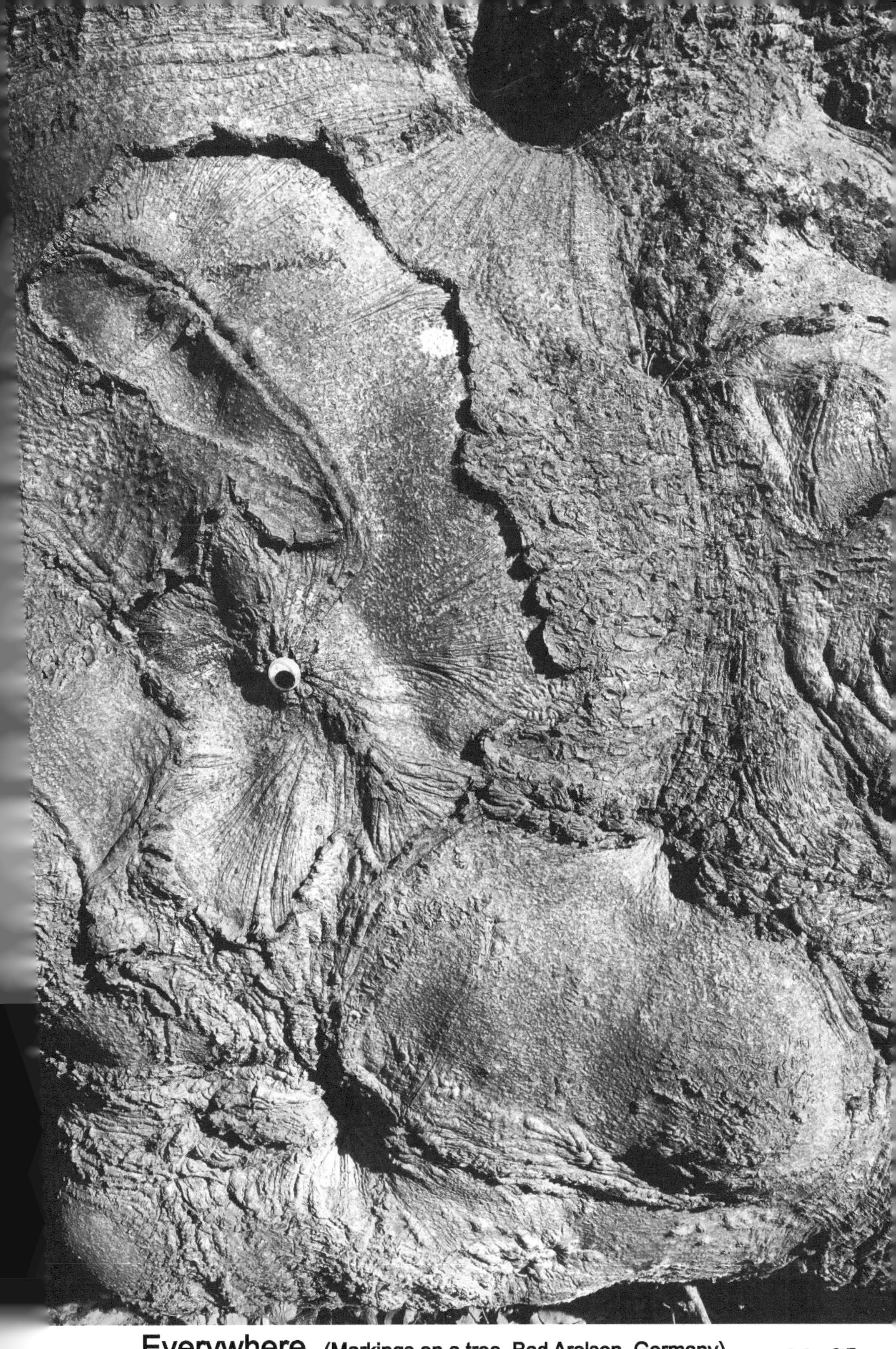

**Everywhere**  (Markings on a tree, Bad Arolsen, Germany)   35

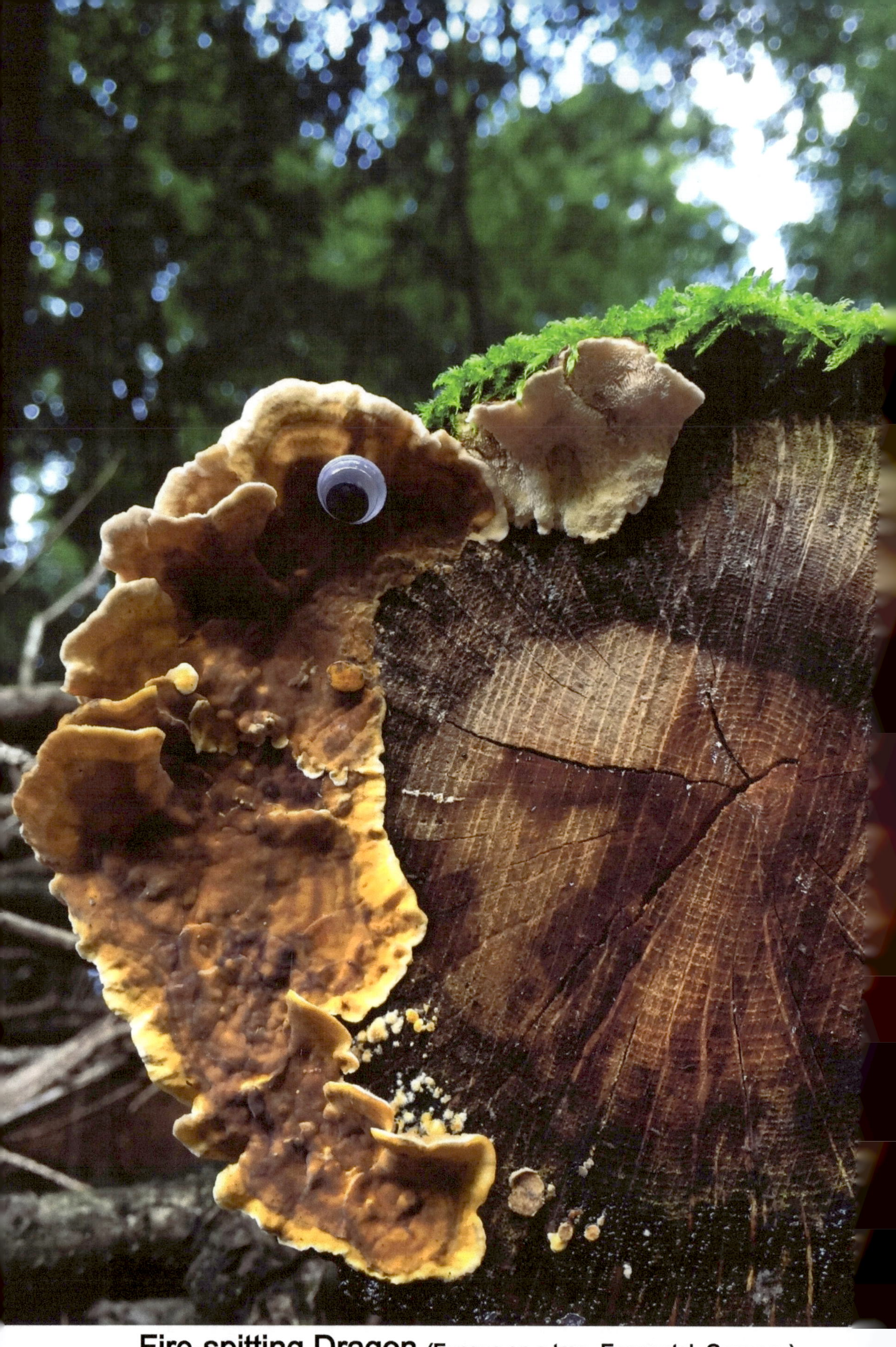

**Fire-spitting Dragon** (Fungus on a tree, Ennepetal, Germany)

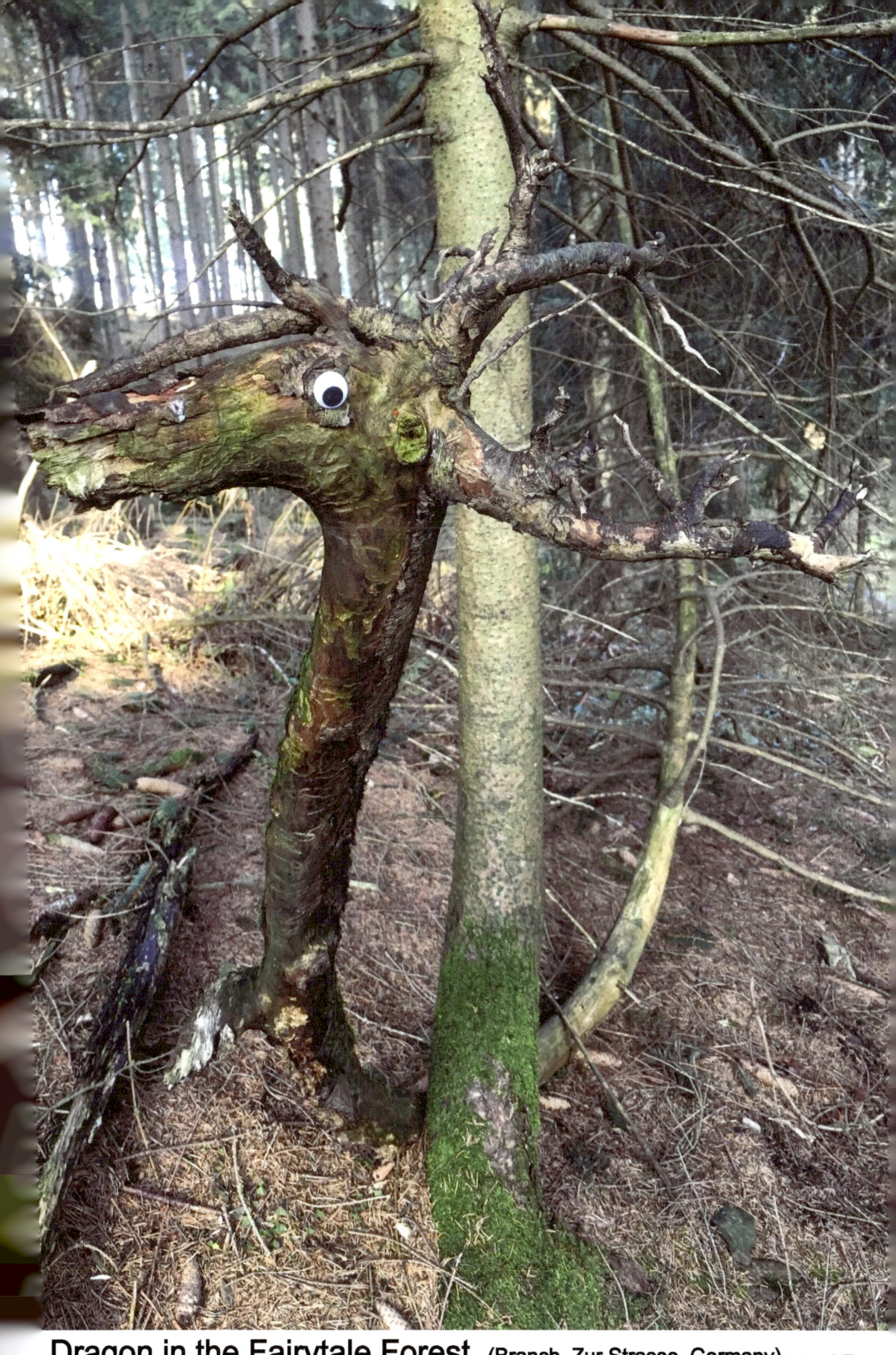

**Dragon in the Fairytale Forest** (Branch, Zur Strasse, Germany) 37

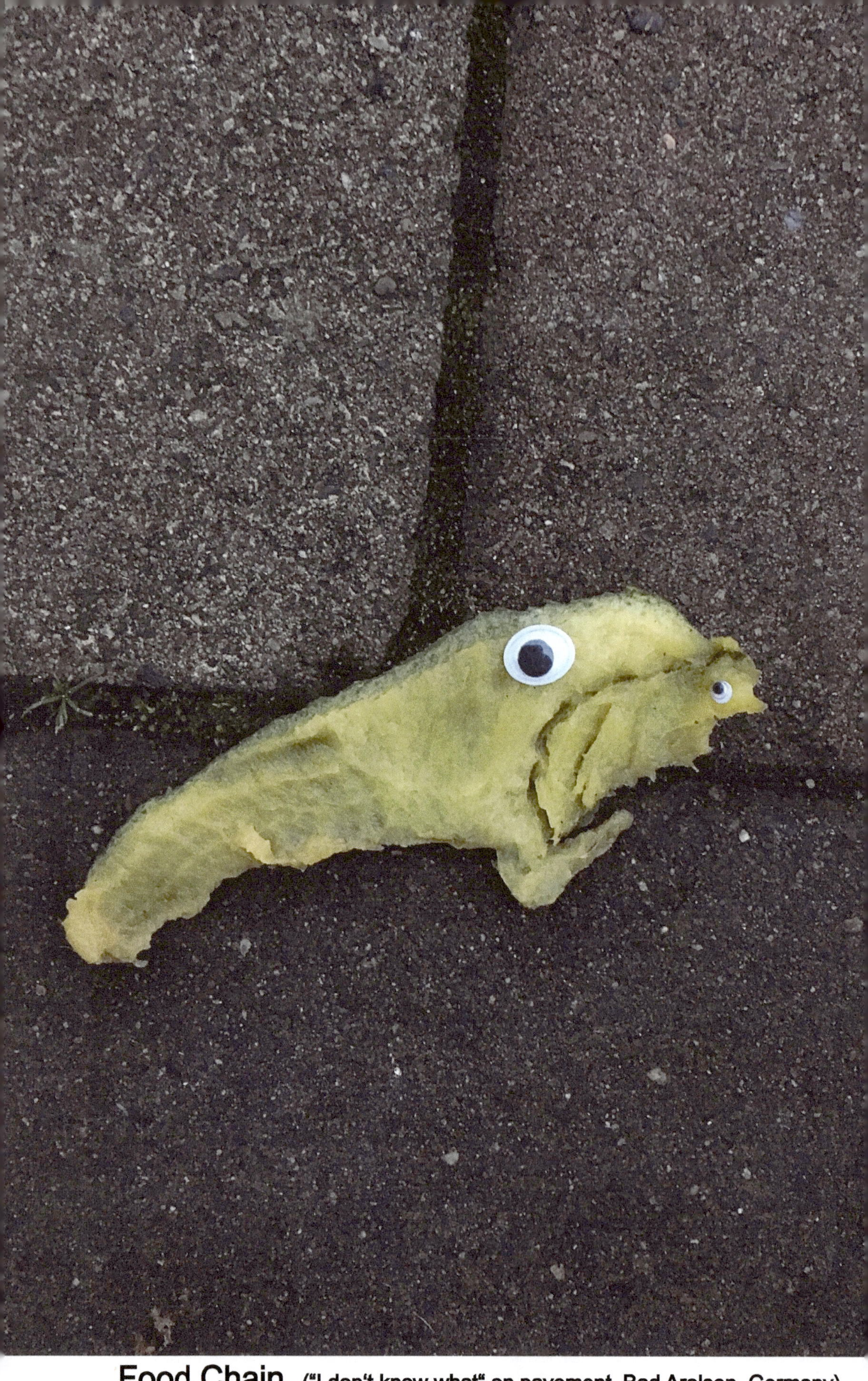

**Food Chain**  ("I don't know what" on pavement, Bad Arolsen, Germany)

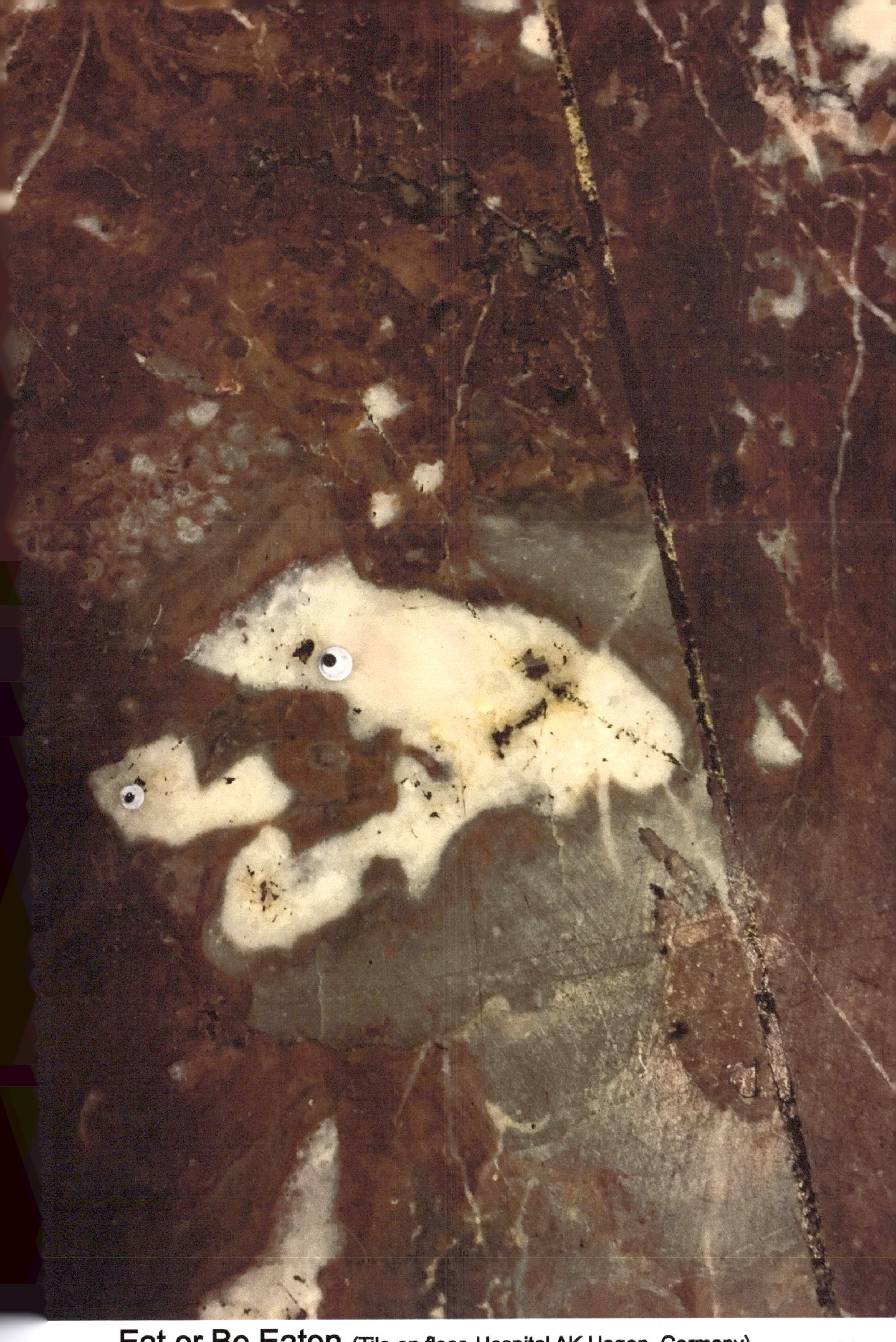

**Eat or Be Eaten** (Tile on floor, Hospital AK Hagen, Germany)   39

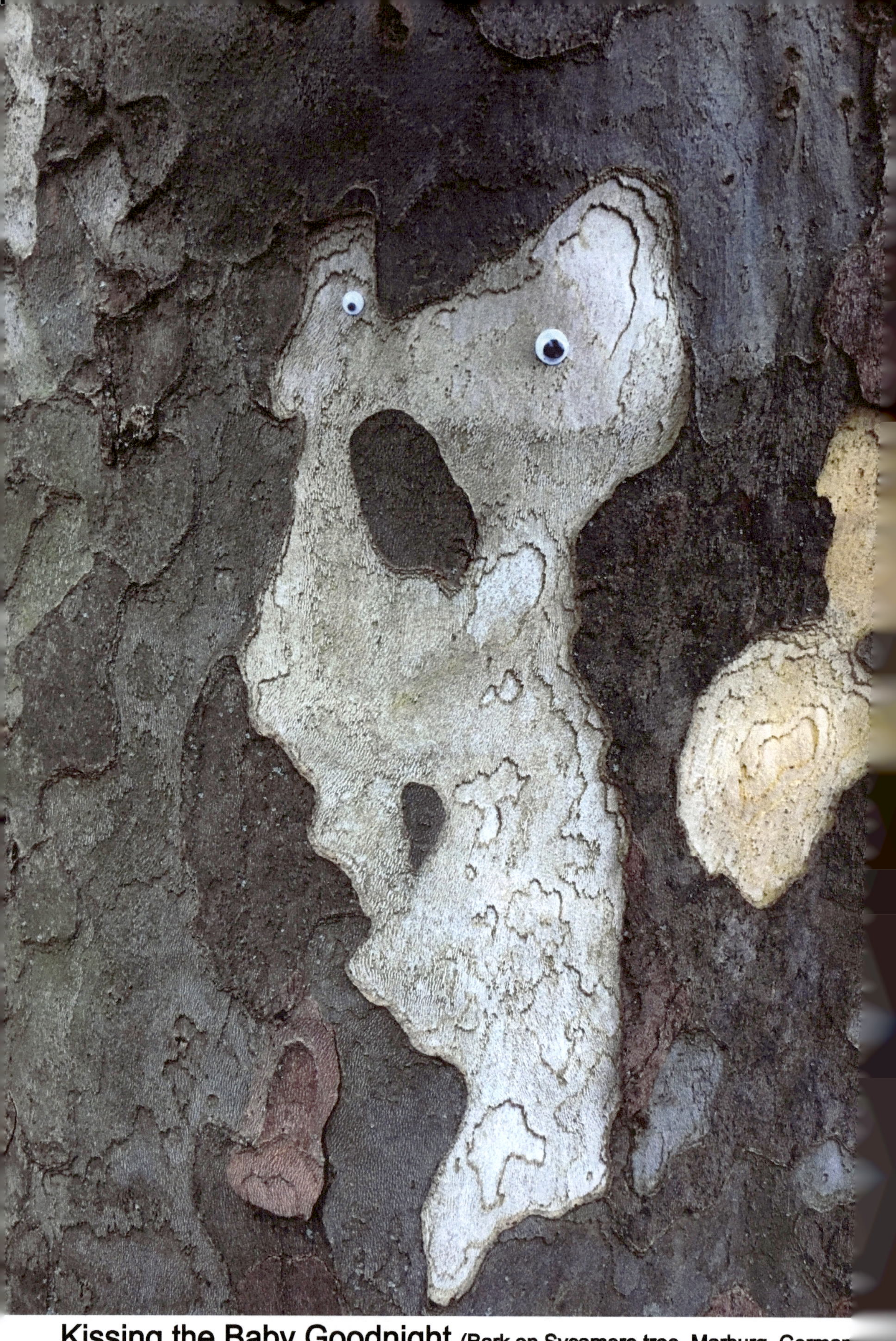

**Kissing the Baby Goodnight** (Bark on Sycamore tree, Marburg, German

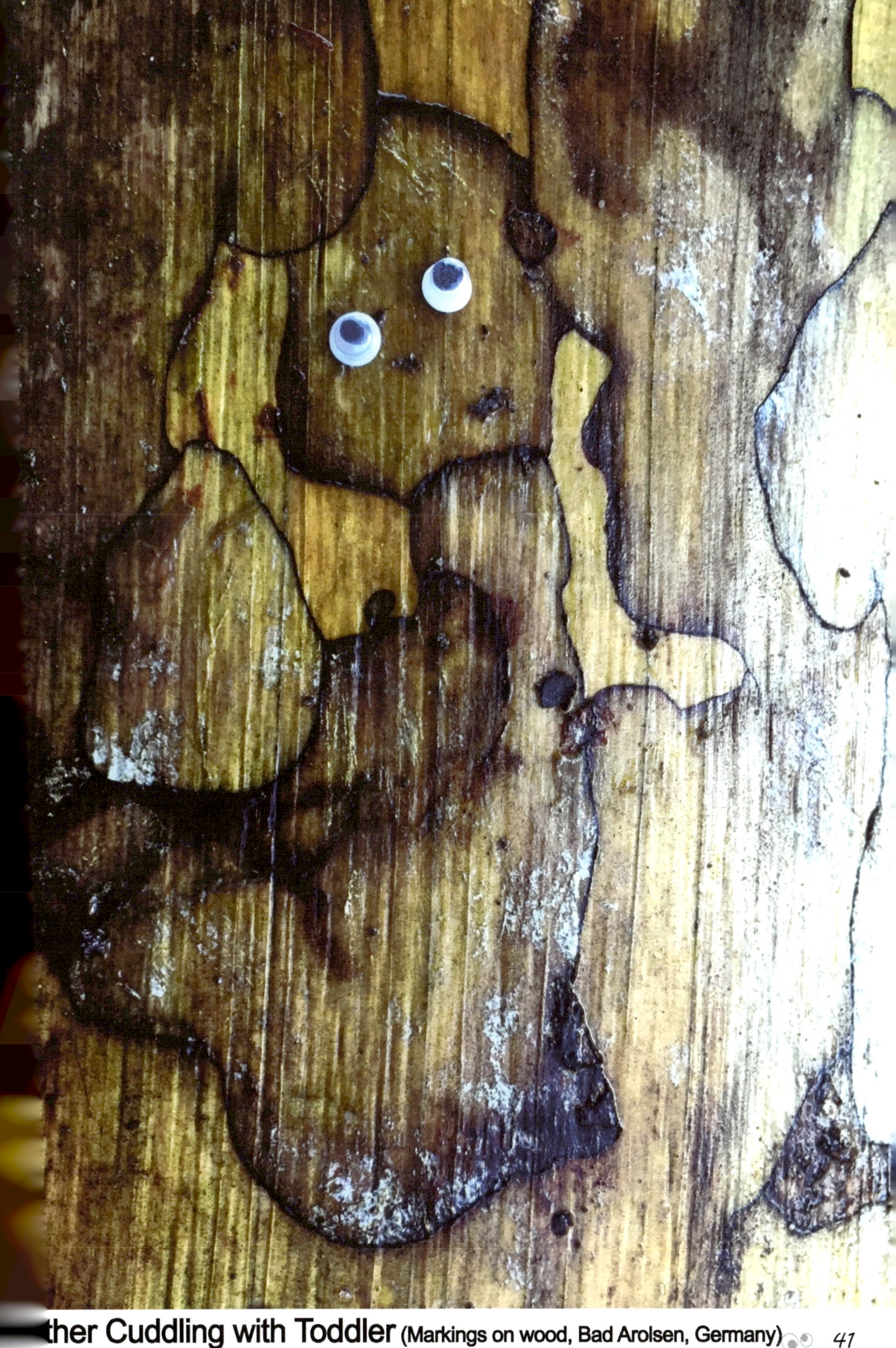

**ther Cuddling with Toddler** (Markings on wood, Bad Arolsen, Germany) 41

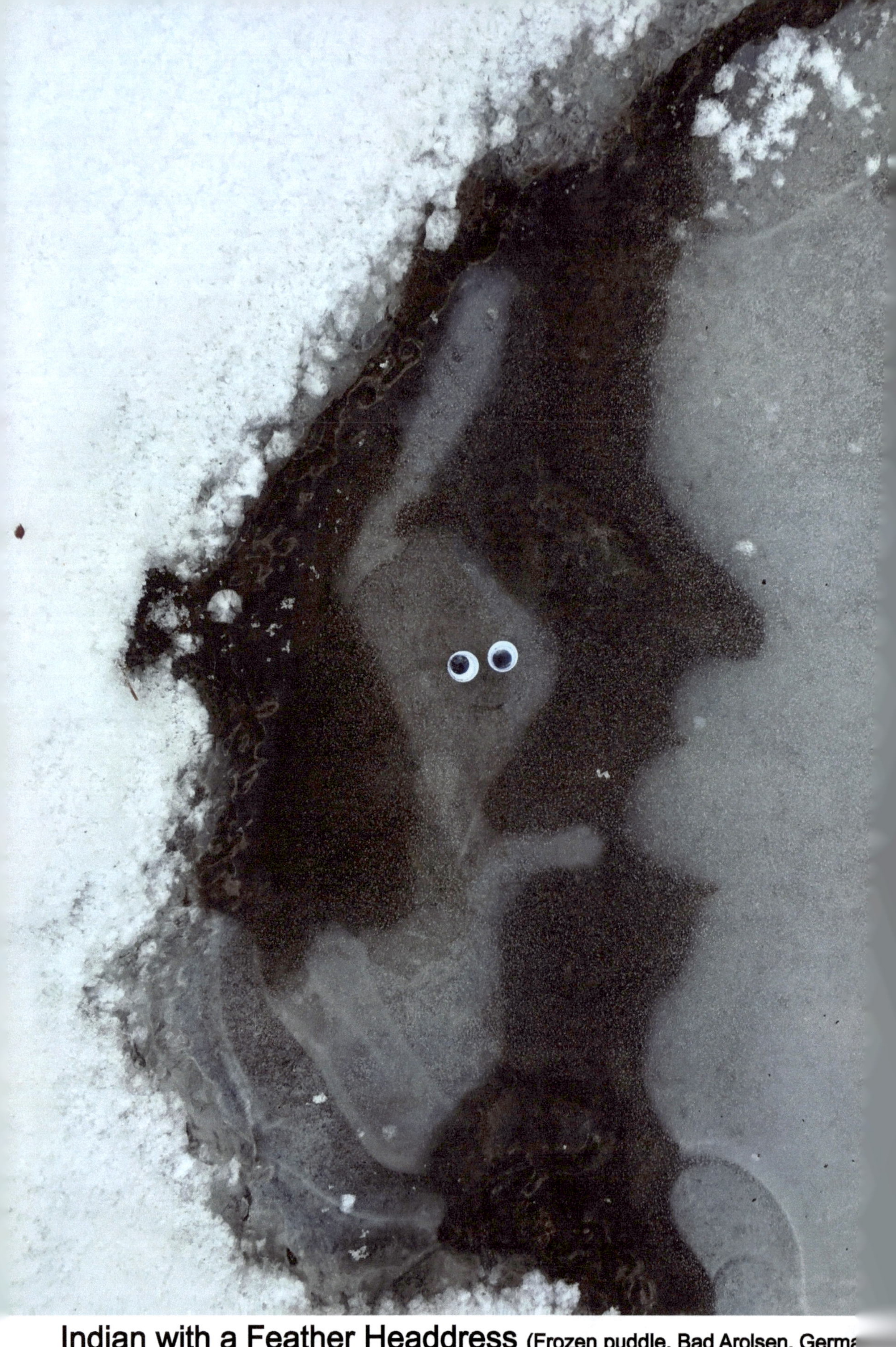

**Indian with a Feather Headdress** (Frozen puddle, Bad Arolsen, Germa

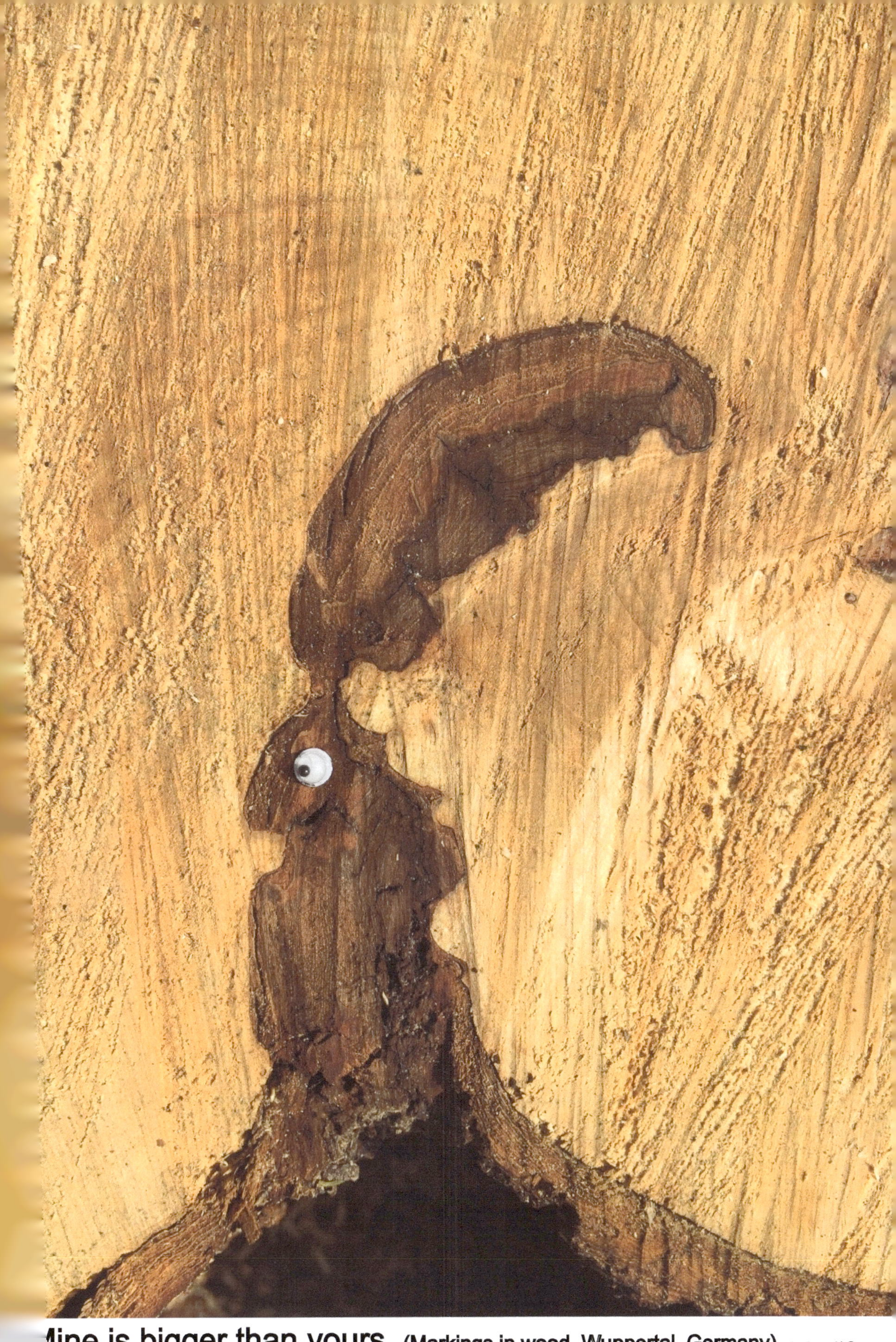

**Mine is bigger than yours** (Markings in wood, Wuppertal, Germany) 👀 *43*

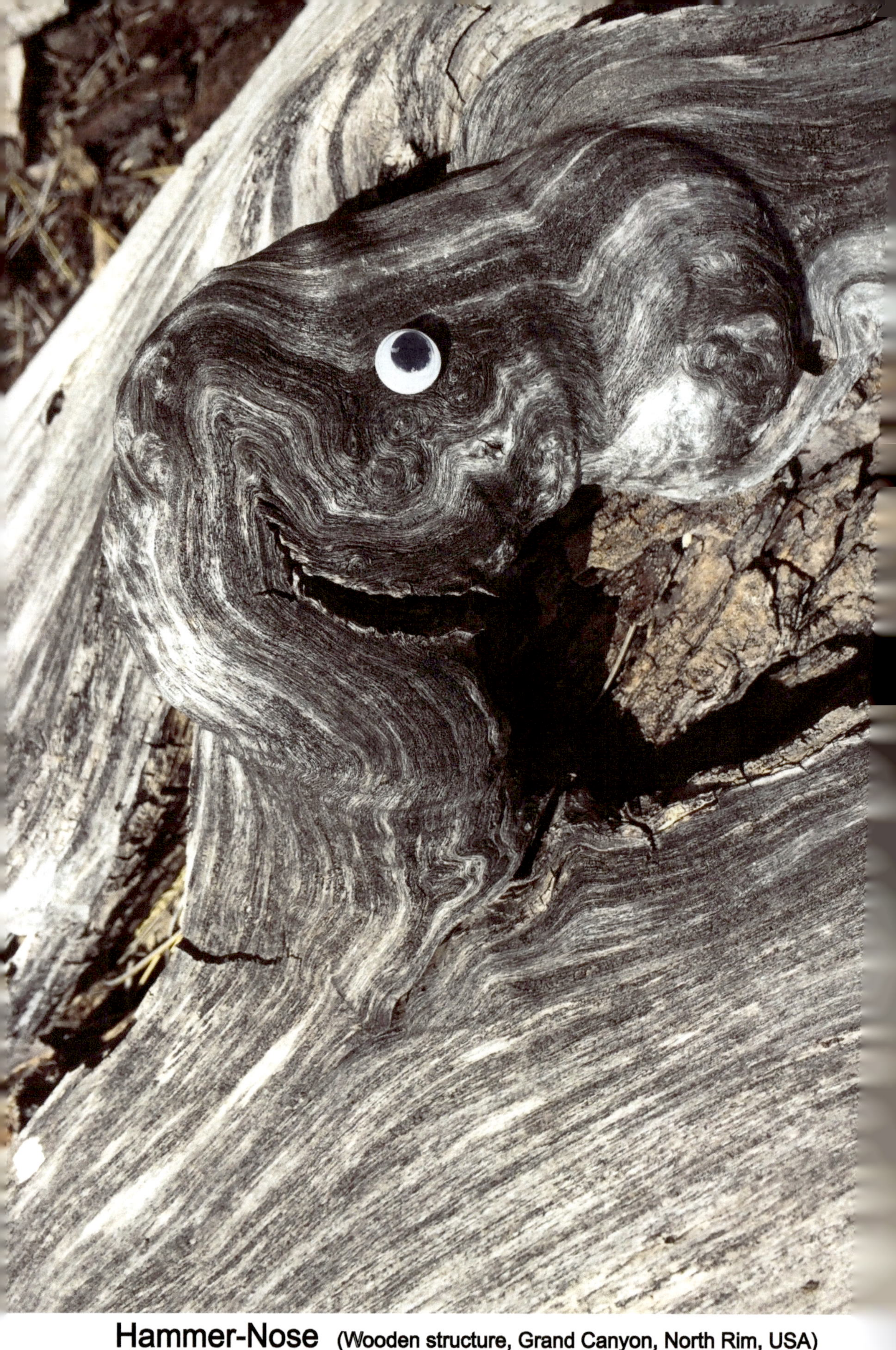

**Hammer-Nose**  (Wooden structure, Grand Canyon, North Rim, USA)

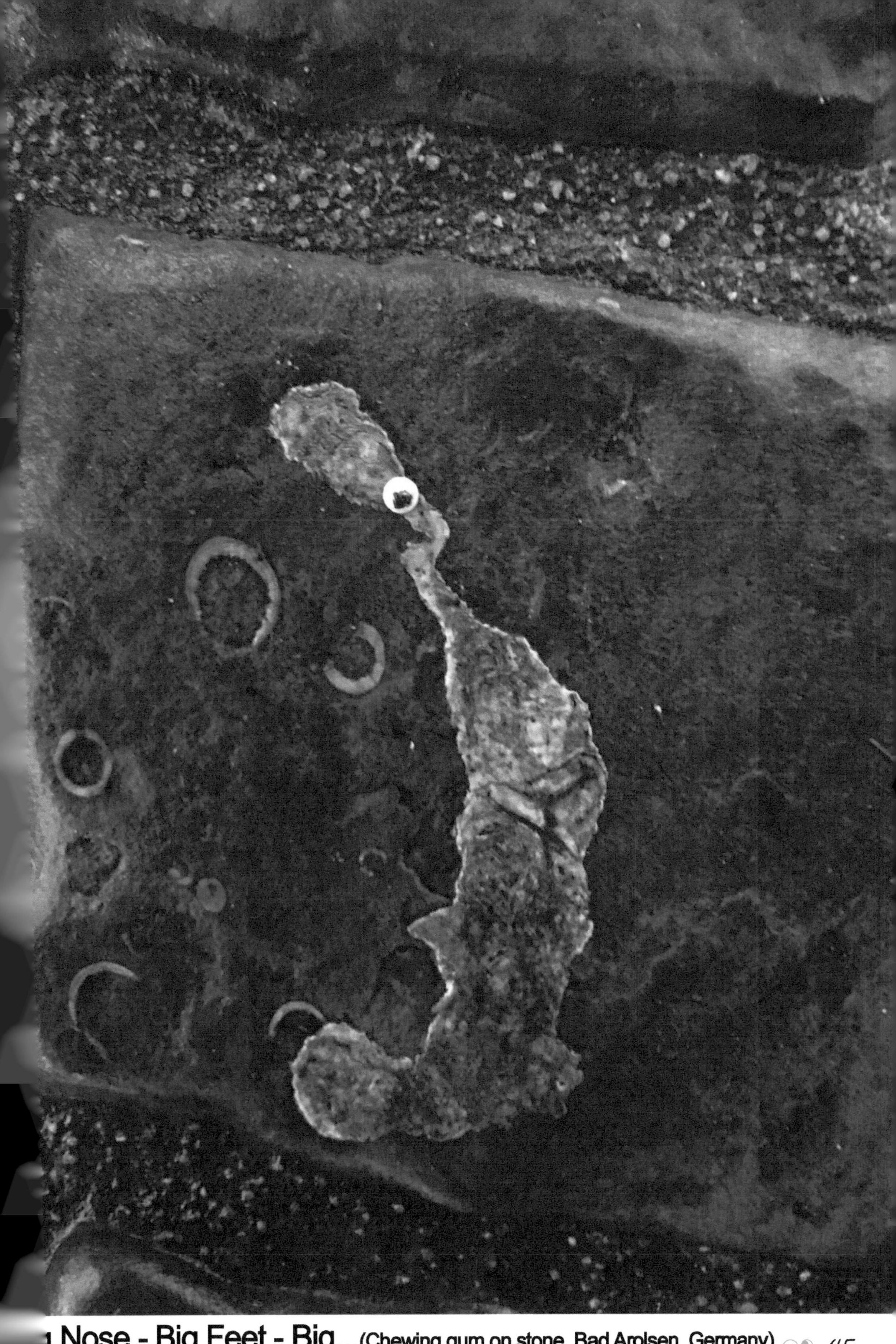

Nose - Big Feet - Big...(Chewing gum on stone, Bad Arolsen, Germany) 45

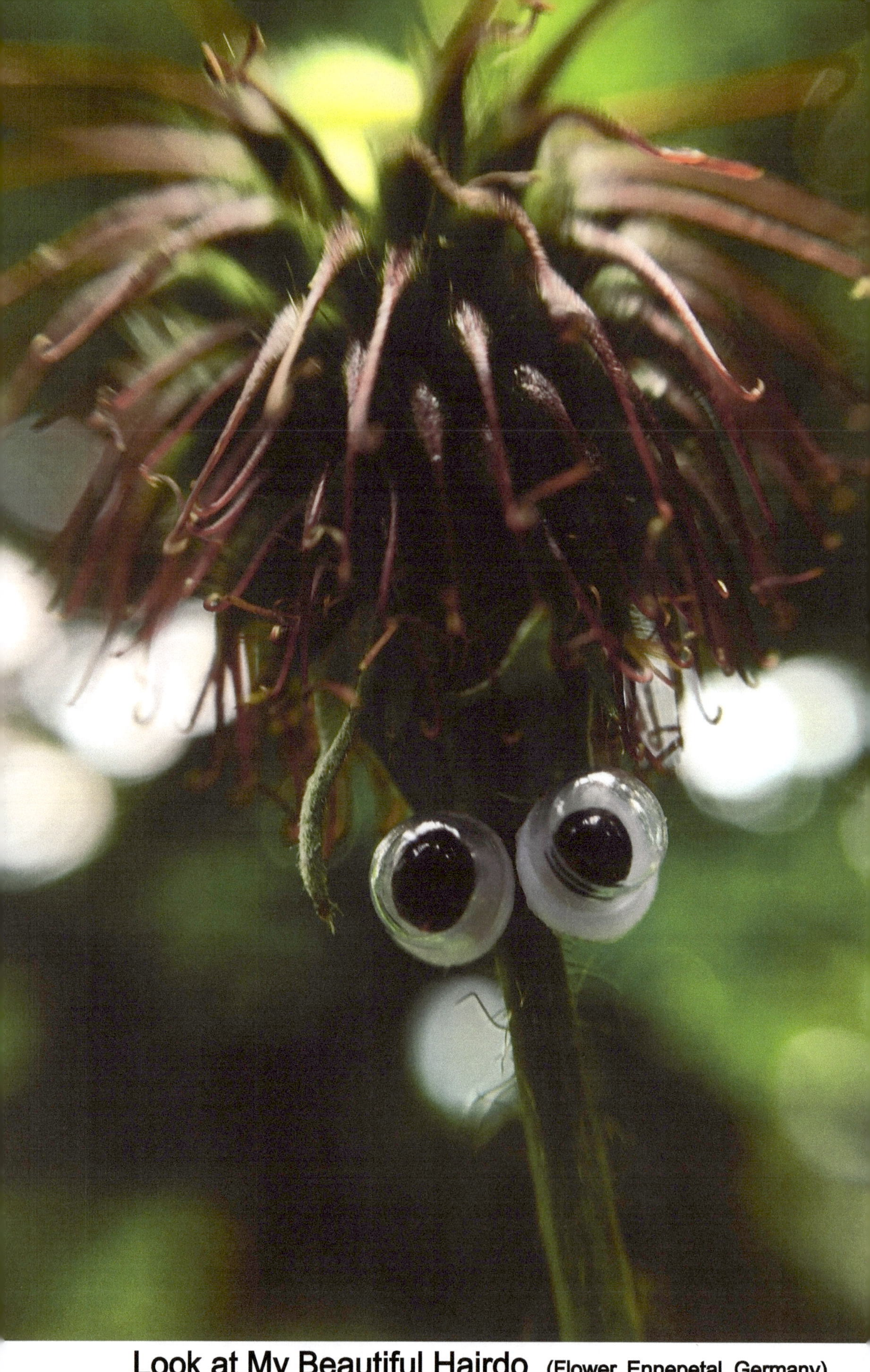

## Look at My Beautiful Hairdo (Flower, Ennepetal, Germany)

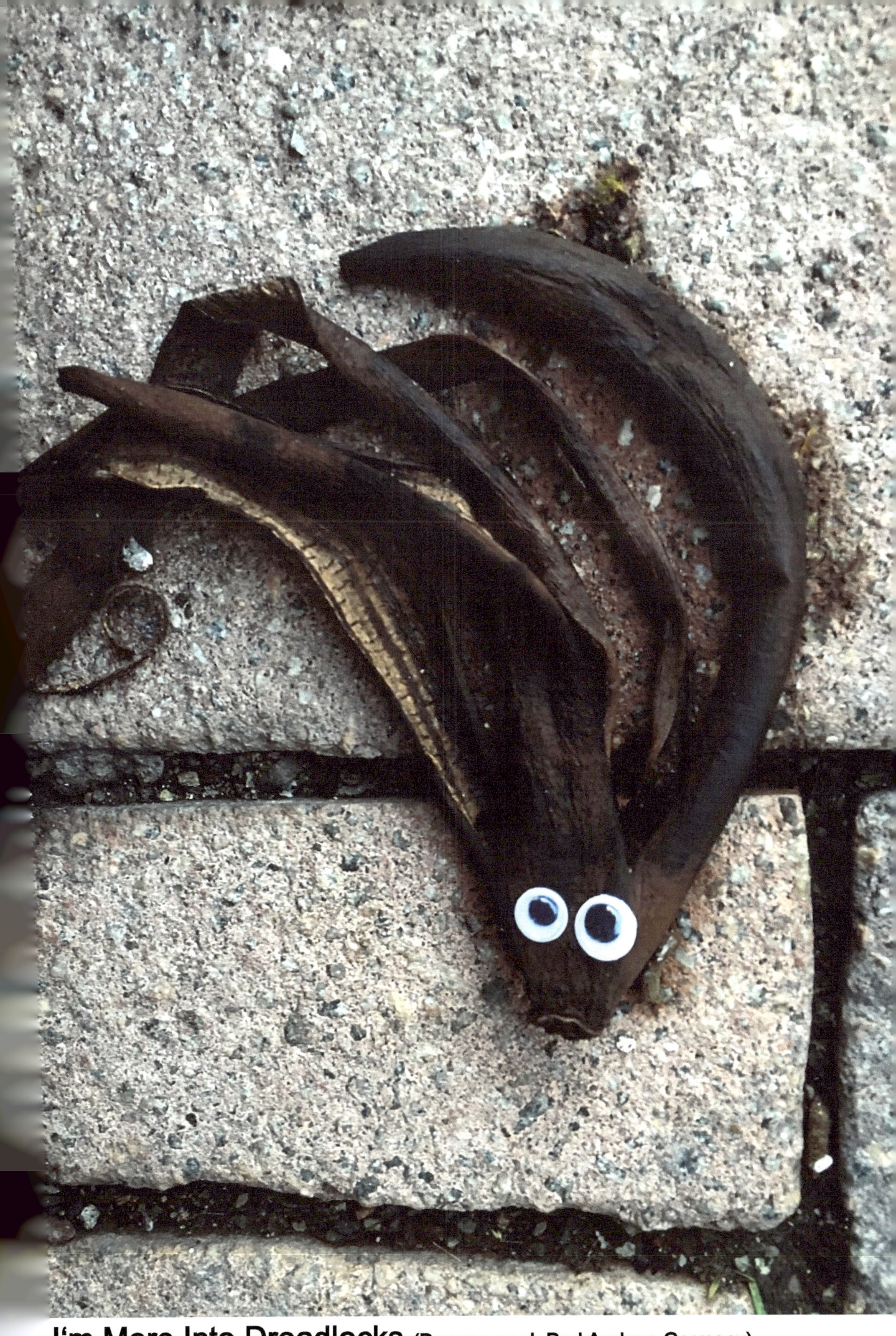

I'm More Into Dreadlocks (Banana peel, Bad Arolsen Germany)

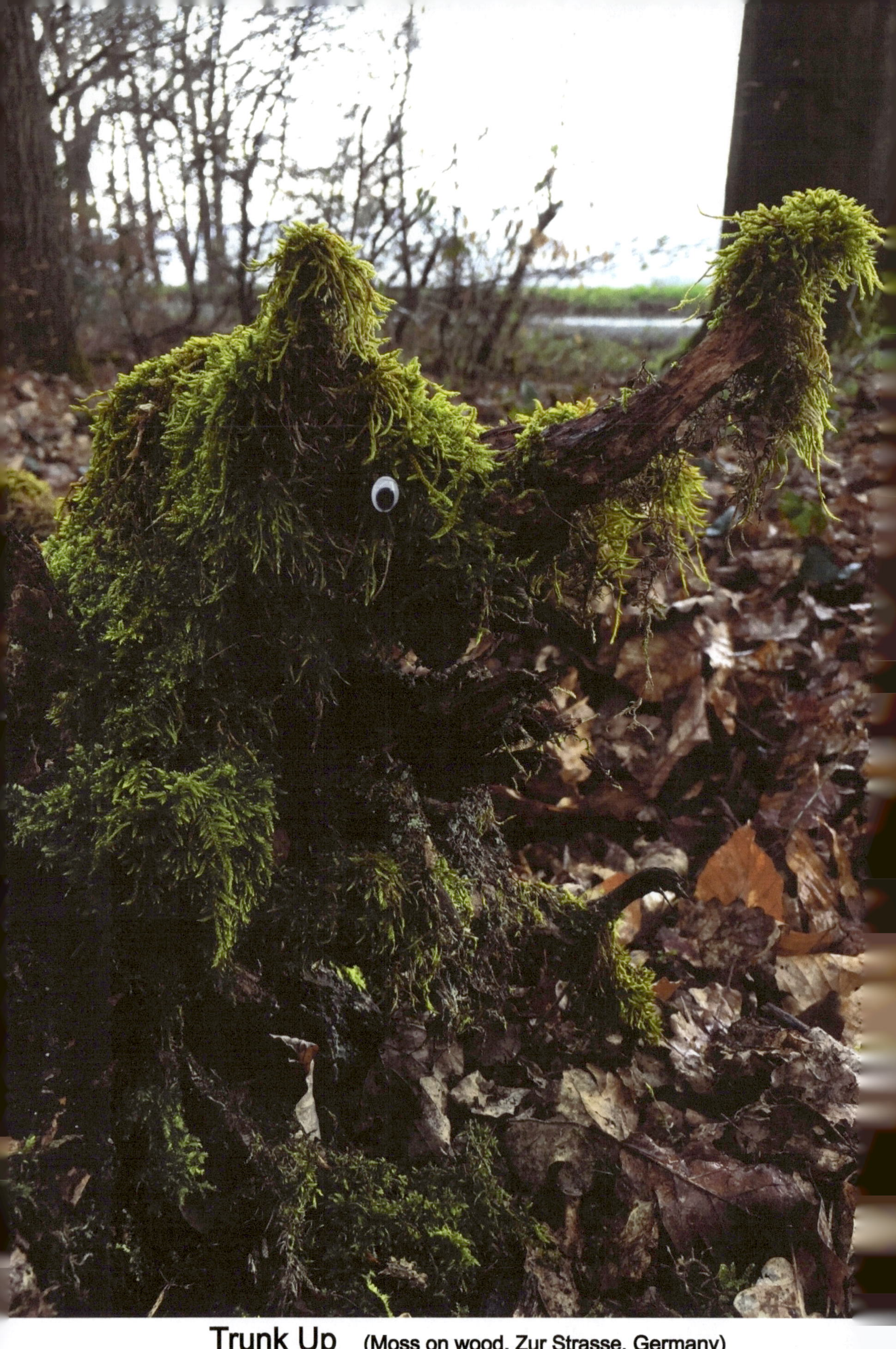

**Trunk Up**   (Moss on wood, Zur Strasse, Germany)

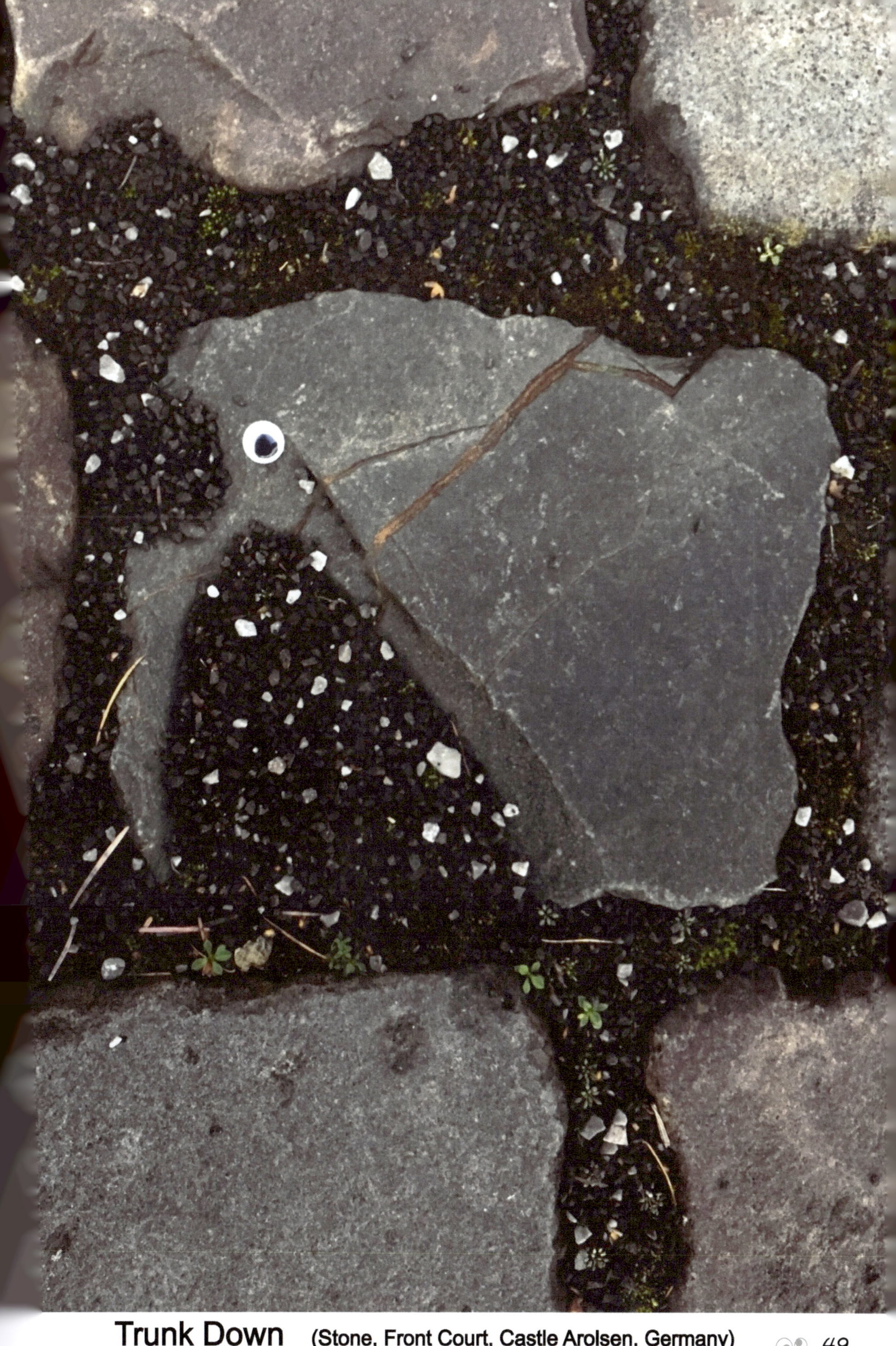

**Trunk Down**    (Stone, Front Court, Castle Arolsen, Germany)

So sad.
This is the last page.

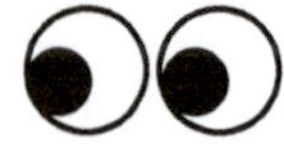

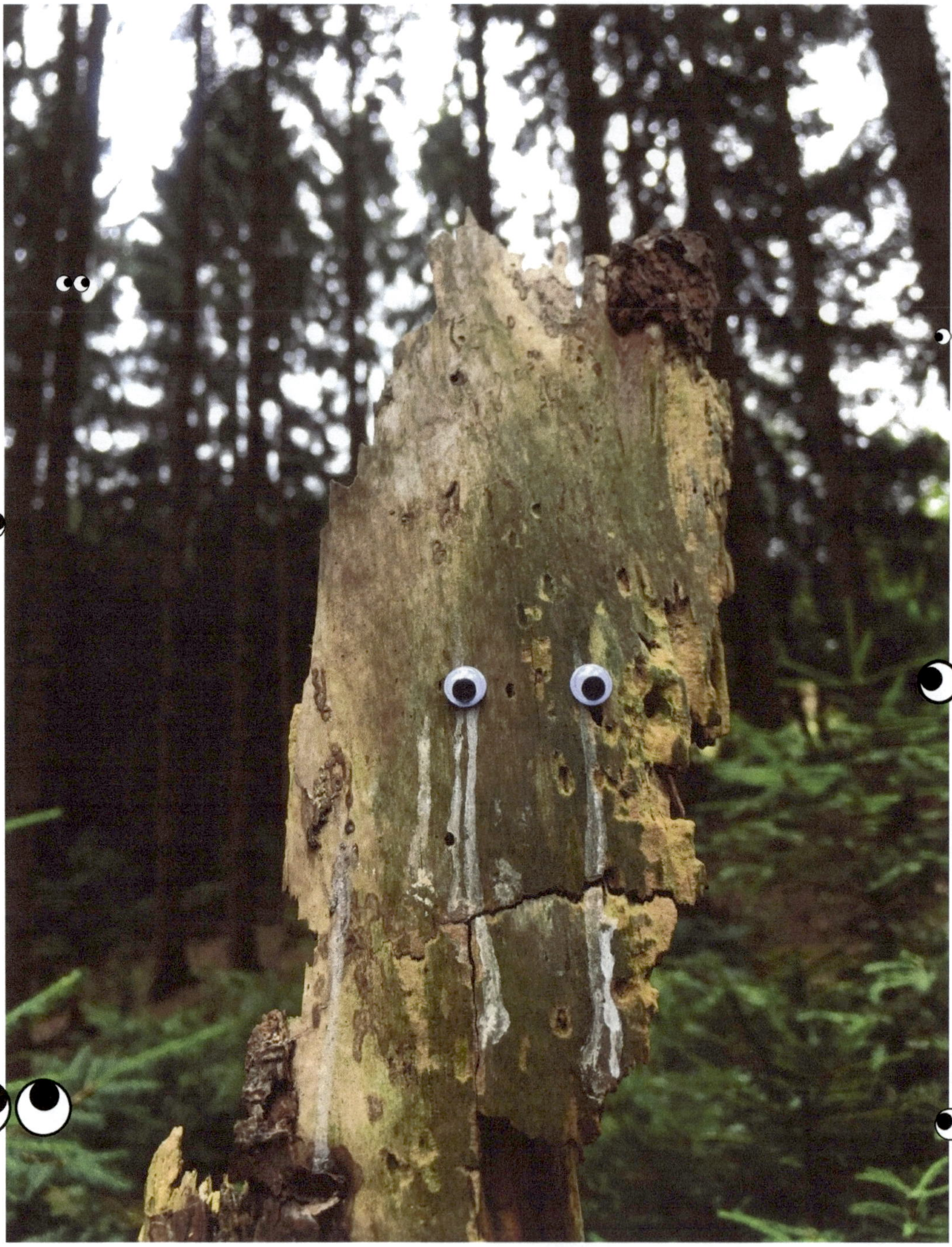

More products at: www.MitAnderenAugen.eu

More books at www.amazon.com.
Search for 'Imke Braselmann' :)

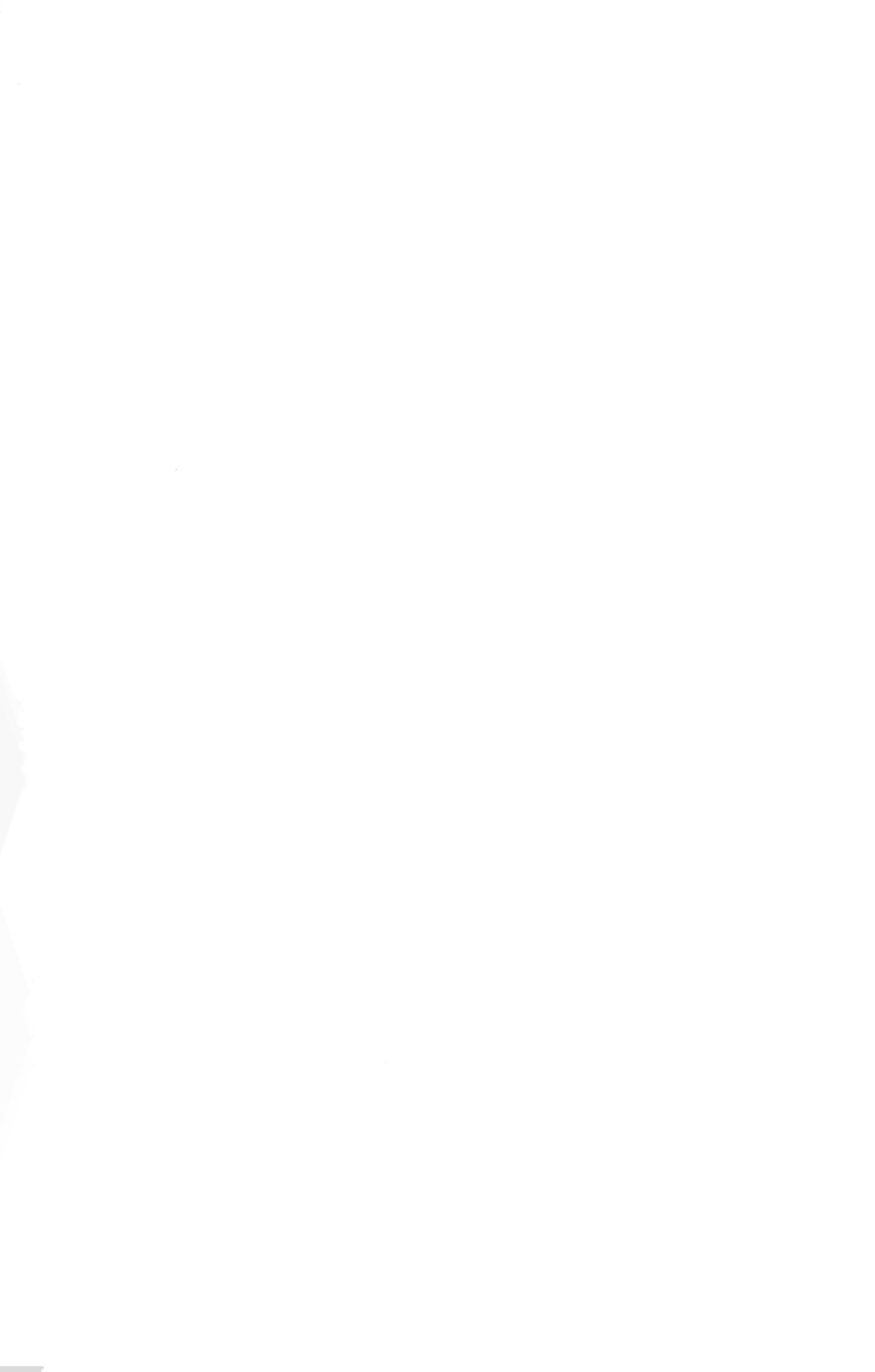